IRAN

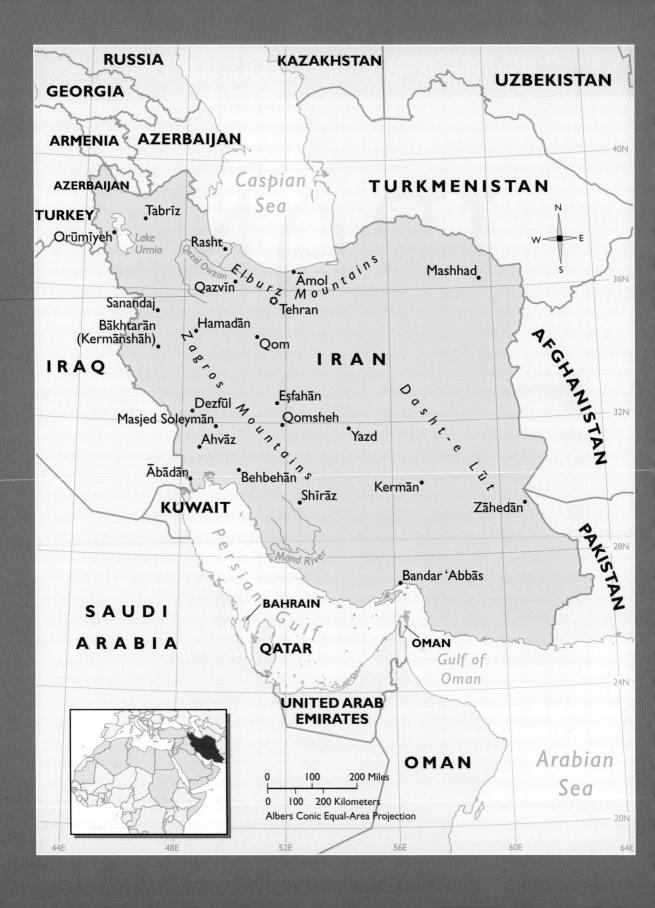

IRAN

William Mark Habeeb

 MASON CREST
PHILADELPHIA

Mason Crest
450 Parkway Drive, Suite D
Broomall, PA 19008
www.masoncrest.com

©2016 by Mason Crest, an imprint of National Highlights, Inc.

Printed and bound in the United States of America.

CPSIA Compliance Information: Batch #MNMME2016.
For further information, contact Mason Crest at 1-866-MCP-Book.

3 5 7 9 8 6 4

Library of Congress Cataloging-in-Publication Data
        on file at the Library of Congress

        978-1-4222-3441-9 (hc)
        978-1-4222-8434-6 (ebook)

Major Nations of the Modern Middle East series ISBN: 978-1-4222-3438-9

TABLE OF CONTENTS

MAJOR NATIONS OF THE MODERN MIDDLE EAST

Afghanistan	Lebanon
Egypt	Pakistan
Iran	The Palestinians
Iraq	Saudi Arabia
Israel	Syria
Jordan	Turkey
The Kurds	

KEY ICONS TO LOOK FOR:

Words to Understand: These words with their easy-to-understand definitions will increase the reader's understanding of the text, while building vocabulary skills.

Sidebars: This boxed material within the main text allows readers to build knowledge, gain insights, explore possibilities, and broaden their perspectives by weaving together additional information to provide realistic and holistic perspectives.

Research Projects: Readers are pointed toward areas of further inquiry connected to each chapter. Suggestions are provided for projects that encourage deeper research and analysis.

Text-Dependent Questions: These questions send the reader back to the text for more careful attention to the evidence presented there.

Series Glossary of Key Terms: This back-of-the book glossary contains terminology used throughout this series. Words found here increase the reader's ability to read and comprehend higher-level books and articles in this field.

Introduction

by Camille Pecastaing, Ph.D.

Oil shocks, wars, terrorism, nuclear proliferation, military and autocratic regimes, ethnic and religious violence, riots and revolutions are the most frequent headlines that draw attention to the Middle East. The region is also identified with Islam, often in unflattering terms. The creed is seen as intolerant and illiberal, oppressive of women and minorities. There are concerns that violence is not only endemic in the region, but also follows migrants overseas. All clichés contain a dose of truth, but that truth needs to be placed in its proper context. The turbulences visited upon the Middle East that grab the headlines are only the symptoms of a deep social phenomenon: the demographic transition. This transition happens once in the life of a society. It is the transition from the agrarian to the industrial age, from rural to urban life, from illiteracy to mass education, all of which supported by massive population growth. It is this transition that fueled the recent development of East Asia, leading to rapid social and economic modernization and to some form of democratization there. It is the same transition that, back in the 19th century, inspired nationalism and socialism in Europe, and that saw the excesses of imperialism, fascism, and Marxist-Leninism. The demographic transition is a period of high risks and great opportunities, and the challenge for the Middle East is to fall on the right side of the sword.

In 1950, the population of the Middle East was about 100 million; it passed 250 million in 1990. Today it exceeds 400 million, to reach about 700 million by 2050. The growth of urbanization is rapid, and concentrated on the coasts and along the few rivers. 1950 Cairo, with an estimated population of 2.5 million, grew into Greater Cairo, a metropolis of about 18 million people. In the same period, Istanbul went from one to 14 million. This expanding populace was bound to test the social system, but regimes were unwilling to take chances with the private sector, reserving for the state a prominent place in the economy. That model failed, population grew faster than the economy, and stress fractures already appeared in the 1970s, with recurrent riots following IMF adjustment programs and the emergence of radical Islamist movements. Against a backdrop of military coups and social unrest, regimes consolidated their rule by subsidizing basic commodities, building up patronage networks (with massive under-employment in a non-productive public sector), and cementing autocratic practices. Decades of continuity in political elites between 1970 and 2010 gave the impression that they had succeeded. The Arab spring shattered that illusion.

The Arab spring exposed a paradox that the Middle East was both one, yet also diverse. Arab unity was apparent in the contagion: societies inspired other societies in a revolutionary wave that engulfed the region yet remained exclusive to it. The rebellious youth was the same; it watched the same footage on al Jazeera and turned to the same online social networks. The claims were the same: less corruption, less police abuse, better standards of living, and off with the tyrants. In some cases, the struggle was one: Syria became a global battlefield, calling young fighters from all around the region to a common cause. But there were differences in the way states fared during the Arab spring. Some escaped unscathed; some got by with a burst of public spending or a sprinkling of democratic reforms, and others yet collapsed into civil wars. The differential resilience of the regimes owes to both the strength and cohesiveness of the repressive apparatus, and the depth of the fiscal cushion they could tap into to buy social peace. Yemen, with a GDP per capita of $4000 and Qatar, at $94,000, are not the same animal. It also became apparent that, despite shared frustrations and a common cause, protesters and insurgents were extremely diverse.

Some embraced free-market capitalism, while others clamored for state welfare to provide immediate improvements to their standards of living. Some thought in terms of country, while other questioned that idea. The day after the Arab spring, everyone looked to democracy for solutions, but few were prepared to invest in the grind of democratic politics. It also quickly became obvious that the competition inherent in democratic life would tear at the social fabric. The few experiments with free elections exposed the formidable polarization between Islamists and non-Islamists. Those modern cleavages paralleled ancient but pregnant divisions. Under the Ottoman Millet system, ethnic and sectarian communities had for centuries coexisted in relative, self-governed segregation. Those communities remained a primary feature of social life, and in a dense, urbanized environment, fractures between Christians and Muslims, Shi'as and Sunnis, Arabs and Berbers, Turks and Kurds were combustible. Autocracy had kept the genie of divisiveness in the bottle. Democracy unleashed it.

This does not mean democracy has to forever elude the region, but that in countries where the state concentrates both political and economic power, elections are a polarizing zero-sum game—even more so when public patronage has to be cut back because of chronic budget deficits. The solution is to bring some distance between the state and the national economy. If all goes well, a growing private sector would absorb the youth, and generate taxes to balance state budgets. For that, the Middle East needs just enough democracy to mitigate endemic corruption, to protect citizens from abuse and extortion, and to allow greater transparency over public finances and over licensing to crony privateers.

Better governance is necessary but no sufficient. The region still needs to figure out a developmental model and find its niche in the global economy. Unfortunately, the timing is not favorable. Mature economies are slow growing, and emerging markets in Asia and Africa are generally more competitive than the Middle East. To succeed, the region has to leverage its assets, starting with its geographic location between Europe, Africa, and Asia. Regional businesses and governments are looking to anchor themselves in south-south relationships. They see the potential clientele of hundreds of millions in Africa and South Asia reaching middle class status, many of whom Muslim. The Middle East can also count on its vast sources of energy, and on the capital accumulated during years of high oil prices. Financial investments in specific sectors, like transport, have already made local companies like Emirates Airlines and DP World global players.

With the exception of Turkey and Israel, the weakness is human capital, which is either unproductive for lack of adequate education, or uncompetitive, because wage expectations in the region are relatively higher than in other emerging economies. The richer Arab countries have worked around the problem by importing low-skilled foreign labor—immigrants who notoriously toil for little pay and even less protection. In parallel, they have made massive investments in higher education, so that the productivity of their native workforce eventually reaches the compensations they expect. For lack of capital, the poorer Arab countries could not follow that route. Faced with low capitalization, sticky wages and high unemployment, they have instead allowed a shadow economy to grow. The arrangement keeps people employed, if at low levels of productivity, and in a manner that brings no tax revenue to the state.

Overall, the commerce of the region with the rest of the world is unhealthy. Oil exporters tend to be one-product economies highly vulnerable to fluctuations in global prices. Labor-rich countries depend too much on remittances from workers in the European Union and the oil-producing countries of the Gulf. Some of the excess labor has found employment in the jihadist sector, a high-risk but up and coming industry which pays decent salaries. For the poorer states of the region, jihadists are the ticket to foreign strategic rent. The Middle East got a taste for it in the early days of the Cold War, when either superpower provided aid to those who declared themselves in their camp. Since then, foreign strategic rent has come in many forms: direct military aid, preferential trade agreements, loan guarantees, financial assistance, or aid programs to cater to refugee populations. Rent never amounts to more than a few percentage points of GDP, but it is often enough to keep entrenched regimes in power. Dysfunction becomes self-perpetuating: pirates and jihadists, famine and refugees, all bear promises of aid to come from concerned distant powers. Reforms lose their urgency.

Turkey and Israel have a head start on the path to modernization and economic maturity, but they are, like the rest of the Middle East, consumed in high stakes politics that hinder their democratic life. Rather than being models that would lift others, they are virtually outliers disconnected from the rest of the region. The clock is ticking for the Middle East. The window of opportunity from the demographic transition will eventually close. Fertility is already dropping, and as the current youth bulge ages it will become a burden on the economy. The outlook for capital is also bleak. Oil is already running out for the smaller producers, all the while global prices are pushed downwards by the exploitation of new sources. The Middle East has a real possibility to break the patterns of the past, but the present is when the transition should occur.

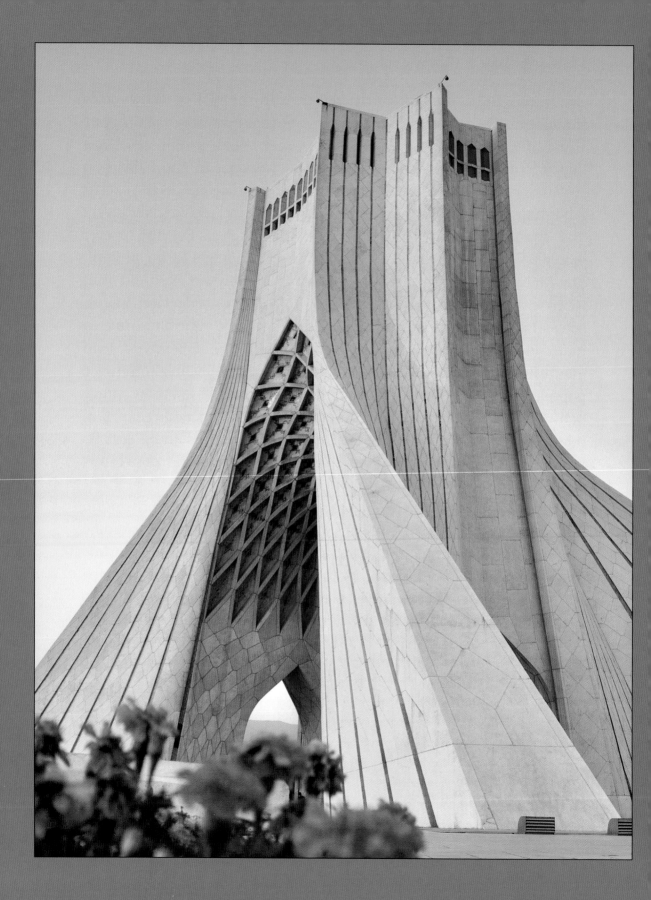

The Azadi ("Freedom") Tower in Tehran is one of the city's best-known landmarks. It is located in Azadi Square, which historically has been the location of mass protests against the Iranian government, most recently during 2009-10.

Place in the World

I ran is home to one of the world's oldest cultures. Known as Persia in ancient times, it was the seat of several powerful empires that, at their height, ruled much of the ancient world. Iran's enduring importance has been in part geographical—it sits at the crossroads of the Middle East, south Asia, and central Asia—and in part cultural, for the ancient Persians not only played an important role in world history, they also made amazing contributions in the fields of art, architecture, and literature. Many of the great monuments and buildings of ancient and medieval Persia still stand, to be admired by modern-day Iranians and visitors alike.

STRATEGIC, RELIGIOUS, AND CULTURAL IMPORTANCE

Because of its strategic location, Iran has always felt the influence of other cultures—particularly the Greeks, Turks, Romans, Mongols, and Arabs—and over time has integrated many of the cultural, social, and political attributes of these other peoples. But Iranian culture and ideas have also influenced Iran's neighbors. For example, even before the introduction of Islam in the seventh century CE, Iran was a major religious center. The Zoroastrian religion, which was founded in Iran, was one of the earliest **monotheistic** faiths and had an important influence on the development of Judaism, Christianity, and Islam.

After the introduction of Islam, Iran quickly rose to a prominent position within the Muslim world as a center of religious learning and study. Iran's genius in the arts and architecture shifted from the building of great palaces for Persian kings to the construction of equally magnificent **mosques** and other religious buildings.

Until about 100 years ago, the lives of most Iranians had changed little since ancient times. But over the past century, Iran went through one of the most rapid modernizations of any country in history. From a land of farmers and nomads, it has become today a heavily urban country, with a good transportation system, modern buildings, generally good health care, and an educational system that is available to students in all areas of the country. But the rapid change that Iran experienced was unsettling to its people in many ways. Also, the industrial and cultural changes were not matched by political changes or a movement toward democracy, meaning that the people had little voice in the country's development. By the late 1970s, many Iranians had become angry at their **authoritarian** government, while others resented the loss of

Words to Understand in This Chapter

authoritarian—characteristic of a form of rule in which one or a few unelected leaders make all decisions for a society.
monotheistic—characterized by a belief in only one God.
mosque—a Muslim house of worship.
shah—a king or sovereign of Iran.

Iran's traditional culture and the growing influence of Western values. The result was the Iranian Revolution (also called the Islamic Revolution), a mass uprising that overthrew Iran's ruler, the **shah**, but replaced him with an equally authoritarian leadership made up of conservative Islamic clerics.

Today, Iran is once again undergoing an internal struggle. Iranians are trying to reconcile the changes that followed the 1979 Islamic Revolution with the needs and requirements of life in the 21st century. Most Iranians are young, and thus focused on the future. They want to reform many aspects of the Islamic Republic to better reflect a modern world-view, and to introduce greater democracy into the political system. But many of the country's leaders—especially the religious leaders—are from an earlier generation, and they are determined to hold on to power. Iran's future will be decided by the outcome of the current struggle between the mostly religious "conservatives" and the "reformers."

One thing, however, is certain: whichever course Iran pursues, it will always play an important role in both the Middle East and the Islamic world.

 Text-Dependent Questions

1. What was this region of the world called in ancient times?
2. In what year did the Iranian Revolution occur?

 Research Project

What was the Zoroastrian religion? Write a short paper and present it to the class.

From atop a cliff, a visitor surveys one of southern Iran's small ports. Most of the strategically located country, which is larger than Alaska, is composed of rugged terrain, including mountains and deserts.

The Land

Iran, a crossroads between the Middle East and south Asia, is one of th e most strategically located countries in the world. It borders seven countries and has almost 1,900 miles (3,180 kilometers) of coastline along two important bodies of water. To the west, Iran is bordered by Iraq and Turkey. To the north are the young states of Armenia and Azerbaijan, the oil-rich and fiercely contested Caspian Sea, and Turkmenistan. To the east, Iran has long and rugged borders with Afghanistan and Pakistan. And to the south lies the Persian Gulf, a vital transit route for the Middle East's oil resources and a body of water that Iranians have always regarded as their domain. Iran controls the Strait of Hormuz, a narrow passage that connects the Persian Gulf with the ocean waters beyond. The strait is a chokepoint for oil tankers sailing to and from the Gulf.

With an area of about 636,000 square miles (1,650,000 square kilometers), Iran is slightly smaller than Alaska and the 18th-largest country in the world by area. But much of Iran's land area

A village in the Zagros mountains.

is desert or mountain, and a mere 11 percent is considered **arable**, or suitable for farming. Indeed, much of Iran ranges from rugged to downright uninhabitable. More than two-thirds of Iran's approximately 81 million people live in urban areas, and this percentage is rising.

Iran has two principal geographical features: mountain ranges, with associated valleys and plains, and deserts. The central part of the country, known as the Plateau of Iran, contains the deserts as well as the plains and foothills of the mountains.

MOUNTAINS AND DESERTS

Two major mountain ranges and an assortment of lesser ranges dominate Iran's topography and cover about 50 percent of the

Words to Understand in This Chapter

arable—suitable or fit for cultivation and farming.
kavir—a salty, desolate desert.

Mountains cover about half of Iran, and the central and eastern parts of the country are dominated by two deserts, the Dasht-e-Kavir and Dasht-e-Lut. The country's vast oil reserves are concentrated in the coastal plain of Khuzistan.

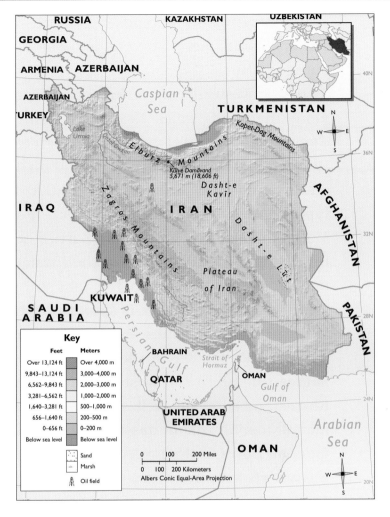

country. The Alborz (or Elburz) Mountains in the north rise steeply from the narrow coastal plain along the southern edge of the Caspian Sea. They contain Iran's highest peak, snow-capped Mount Damavand, an active volcano that rises 18,606 feet (5,671 meters). The Alborz range also contains lush valleys and dense forests, and it is sprinkled with little mountain villages and towns. The coastal plain between the Alborz Mountains and the Caspian Sea enjoys abundant rainfall and is a productive agricultural region, specializing in rice, tea, cotton, and citrus fruits. Iran's capital city, Tehran, is nestled in the southern foothills of the Alborz, and the mountains are popular with vacationing Tehranis.

The Alborz chain extends eastward toward the border with Turkmenistan. Here, streams and oases make the valleys suitable for agriculture.

In the western part of Iran, the Zagros Mountains stretch for more than 600 miles (966 km) from northwest to southeast. Consisting of parallel ridges interspersed with plains and valleys, the Zagros range expands to more than 100 miles (1,600 km) wide and contains five peaks of over 13,000 feet (3,965 meters) before tapering off in southeastern Iran. For centuries, the Zagros Mountains made a formidable barrier between the central part of the country and the waters of the Persian Gulf. There are very few natural passages through the mountains, and even today travel through the Zagros range is slow. Nevertheless, some of Iran's most fabled and ancient cities—including Isfahan (also spelled Esfahan), Yazd, and Persepolis—arose in the plains and foothills between the Zagros ridges. To the west of the Zagros lies the coastal plain of Khuzistan, a region well watered by streams draining from the mountains. Khuzistan has a mild climate and is also the location of much of Iran's vast petroleum reserves.

In northwest Iran, near the borders with Turkey, Armenia, and Azerbaijan, the Zagros and Alborz ranges blend together into lesser ranges. The most important of these are the volcanic Sabalan and Talesh ranges, which include Mount Sabalan, a peak that rises above 15,800 feet (4,819 meters). The many plains and valleys in the northwest are among the most fertile land in Iran.

Most of central and eastern Iran is covered by two huge deserts, the Dasht-e-Kavir and the Dasht-e-Lut. Both were lakebeds in prehistoric times, but today they are barren and inhospitable, and together they cover nearly one-fifth of the country. Dasht-e-Kavir means "salt desert"; it is covered by **kavirs**, which are vast areas of crust-covered salty mud completely devoid of plant or animal life. The Dasht-e-Kavir stretches for about 500 miles (805 km), averaging 200 miles (322 km) in width. Measuring about 300 by 200 miles (483 by 322 km), the smaller Dasht-e-Lut is sandy, windy, dusty, and equally inhospitable. Until fairly recent times, these deserts were virtually impassable, and they remain dangerous to unwary adventurers. People have been known to break through the crust of a *kavir* and drown in the salty muck below.

LAKES AND RIVERS

Iran is not blessed with great rivers: only three in the entire country are of real significance. The Karun, in the southwest, is Iran's only navigable river. More than 500 miles (805 km) in length, it flows westward out of the Zagros Mountains to the Persian Gulf,

 Quick Facts: The Geography of Iran

Location: Middle East, bordering the Gulf of Oman, the Persian Gulf, and the Caspian Sea, between Iraq and Pakistan

Area: (slightly smaller than Alaska)
total: 636,000 square miles (1,648,195 sq km)
land: 591,000 square miles (1,531,595 sq km)
water: 45,000 square miles (116,600 sq km)

Borders: Afghanistan, 572 miles (921 km); Armenia, 27 miles (44 km); Azerbaijan, 428 miles (689 km); Iraq, 994 miles (1,599 km); Pakistan, 596 miles (959 km); Turkey, 332 miles (534 km); Turkmenistan, 713 miles (1,148 km)

Climate: mostly arid or semiarid, subtropical along the Caspian coast

Terrain: rugged, mountainous rim; high, central basin with deserts, mountains; small, discontinuous plains along both coasts

Elevation extremes:
lowest point: Caspian Sea, 90 feet (-28 meters)
highest point: Kuh-e Damavand, 18,606 feet (5,671 meters)

Natural hazards: periodic droughts, floods, dust storms, sandstorms, earthquakes

Source: CIA World Factbook, 2015.

Bandar-e Anzali, on the Caspian Sea, is one of the most important seaports in northern Iran.

providing water for irrigation along the way. On the other side of the Zagros, flowing eastward into the plains, is the Zayandeh River. Its principal significance is that it provides water for the great city of Isfahan. Iran's other important river, the Helmand, originates in Afghanistan and flows through the arid southeastern part of the country near the border with Pakistan, making agriculture possible in this area, which borders the great deserts.

Orumiyeh (also spelled Urmia), Iran's largest lake at 3,700 square miles (9,579 sq km), is located in the extreme northwestern part of the country near the Turkish border. The lake's waters are so salty that no fish can survive in them, and they can't be used for drinking water or irrigation. Another large, marshy, and salty lake, Namak, lies south of Tehran in the Plateau of Iran. The country has very few freshwater lakes.

The salty Caspian Sea is misnamed; it is actually the world's largest lake. In addition to Iran, Russia, Turkmenistan, Azerbaijan, and Kazakhstan border the Caspian Sea. These five countries have held negotiations about how to share the Caspian's resources, which include oil reserves and fish; Caspian caviar (made from the roe, or eggs, of sturgeons) is a world-famous delicacy and fetches enormous sums of money. Iran's Caspian coast has been developed into a major tourist region.

CLIMATE

Iran's climate varies dramatically, from season to season as well as from region to region. It ranges from subtropical (along the Caspian coastal plain) to arctic (in the northwest mountains). In general, however, winters are cold—especially in the mountains—and summers are extremely hot. The deserts are unbearably hot during the day but can be frigid at night. Some of the higher mountains are snow-capped year-round. Iran is mostly arid, or very dry, except for the coastal plain along the Caspian Sea and the northwest, both of which receive significant rainfall. The northwest also receives winter snows and experiences very cold temperatures.

Southern Iran and the Persian Gulf coast are extremely hot and humid in the summer; temperatures above 120° Fahrenheit (49° Celsius) are not uncommon. In the winter, however, these regions can be quite pleasant, with mild temperatures and periodic rainfall.

The non-desert parts of the Iranian plateau enjoy more moderate climate conditions. Tehran, for example, has hot and dry summers, with high temperatures approaching 100°F (39°C), followed by chilly winters, when nighttime temperatures regularly dip below freezing. Tehran receives rain and snow mainly during the winter.

 # Text-Dependent Questions

1. What percentage of Iran's land area is suitable for farming?
2. What is Iran's highest mountain?
3. What is Iran's only navigable river?

 # Research Project

Conduct an online exploration of Iran's *kavirs*. What caused them? Are there routes for crossing them? Find true-life dramas that illustrate the dangers of the *kavirs*.

In ancient times, Iran—then called Persia—was the center of powerful empires. Shown here, near Pasargadae, is the tomb of King Cyrus the Great, the founder of the Persian Achaemenid Empire, who ruled from 550 to 529 BCE.

History

Iran has a rich and fascinating history. Known as Persia until modern times, the country produced several of the ancient world's most powerful empires and most famous emperors. At its grandest, under Cyrus the Great in the sixth century BCE, the Persian Empire stretched from Egypt to India. Over the centuries, imperial Persia's wars with the Greeks, Romans, Ottoman Turks, and Byzantines helped determine the course of history for the entire Mediterranean and Middle East regions.

Periods of imperial expansion were interspersed with invasions from outside. Alexander the Great and Genghis Khan were among those who attacked and occupied Iran in ancient times. But the most important outside influence on Iran came from invading Muslim forces, who by 700 CE had successfully transformed the country into an Islamic nation, which it has remained ever since.

Britain and Russia fought for influence over Iran in the 18th and 19th centuries, and during World War II Iran's oil resources and strategic location made it a prize in the eyes of both Nazi Germany and the Allies. Over most of the past century, Iranian society and politics have been characterized by a struggle between the forces of "modernization" and those, led in large part by religious leaders, who favor Islamic tradition. This struggle came to a head in 1979, when the Islamic cleric **Ayatollah** Ruhollah Khomeini led a revolution that overthrew the pro-Western shah, Iran's ruler. Today, in the Islamic Republic of Iran, the internal struggle between these forces continues, even as Iran plays an increasingly important role on the world stage.

EARLY HISTORY

Archaeological evidence indicates that Iran was settled as long ago as 6000 BCE. Around 1000 BCE, nomadic **Indo-European** tribes from central Asia began to move southward into eastern Iran and the area of the Zagros Mountains. Two of these tribes—the

Words to Understand in This Chapter

ayatollah—the highest-ranking cleric in the Shiite religion.

caliph—the ruler of the Muslim world, whom Shiites believed should be a descendant of Muhammad.

city-state—an independent, sovereign city.

coup—the overthrow of a government or leader through force or the threat of force.

deities—gods or goddesses.

expropriation—the seizure of private property for public use.

hojatoleslam—a mid-level Shia cleric.

Indo-European—one of the major families of languages; or a member of one of the tribal groups that migrated west from central Asia and spoke an early form of these languages.

Majlis—the Iranian parliament.

nationalization—the process by which a government takes control of privately owned property or businesses.

political prisoners—people who are imprisoned because of their political beliefs or actions.

protectorate—a country or land that is under the partial control of another, usually more powerful, country.

sanctions—penalty imposed against one country by others.

satrap—an official in the Persian Empire who administered a province.

secular—not religious.

Medes and the Persians—became the most powerful. The Medes drove the Scythians—another tribal people—out of Iran and engaged in a long war with the great Assyrian Empire to the west. In 612 BCE, the Medes, in alliance with Babylonia, defeated the Assyrians and sacked the Assyrian capital of Nineveh.

Meanwhile, the Persians were solidifying their control in the southern Zagros Mountains. Legend has it that the Persians' first king was Achaemenes, and that his grandson, Cambeses I, married the daughter of the Median king. They had a son, Cyrus II, who was destined to become one of antiquity's greatest and most powerful rulers. Cyrus began by using both force and persuasion to unify the Medes and the Persians into a single powerful nation. Declaring himself "king of kings" and "an Achaemenid" (descendant of Achaemenes), Cyrus the Great, as he came to be known, used his new base of support to create the most extensive empire the world had ever known.

Cyrus's first important victory, around 550 BCE, was over King Croesus of Lydia, who ruled much of what is today Turkey. After securing control of these lands, Cyrus sought to enlarge his empire by attacking Babylonia. The Babylonians, although masters of a great empire themselves, were weakened by internal rivalries, and in 539 BCE their great capital city, Babylon, fell to Cyrus's armies. The Persian king now controlled Turkey, Mesopotamia, and all the lands westward to the Mediterranean and the borders of Egypt.

Cyrus established a royal capital, at Pasargadae in the

Did You Know?

Beginning around 100 BCE, merchants from China traveled eastward to trade their luxurious and valuable silk. The caravan routes they took, which became known as the Silk Road, traversed Iran from the far northeast to the borders with Turkey. During its peak in the 13th and 14th centuries, thousands of traders of different nationalities and religions crossed through Iran carrying silk and spices destined for the Ottoman Empire and European royalty.

(Left) Darius the Great, who expanded the Persian Empire as far east as India and as far north as the Danube River in Europe, ruled over an estimated 50 million subjects. But by the time of his death in 486 BCE, the Greeks had begun to challenge Persian power.

(Right) Persepolis, Darius's capital, was once a magnificent imperial city. When Alexander the Great conquered the Persians in the fourth century BCE, however, he razed the palace complex; much of the rest of the city was destroyed in subsequent earthquakes.

Persian heartland, and adorned it with palaces and monuments. Regarded by many historians as an "enlightened" ruler, Cyrus was apparently gracious in victory, allowing the peoples he conquered to maintain their customs and traditions. He is perhaps most famous for liberating the Hebrew people, who had been held captive in Babylon after the Babylonian conquest of Israel. Cyrus not only allowed the Jews to return to Israel, but he also granted permission for them to rebuild their Holy Temple in Jerusalem.

Cyrus was killed around 529 BCE while battling nomadic tribes. His son further expanded the Persian Empire by conquering Egypt.

But soon afterward the empire descended into a period of chaos, until Darius I—who may or may not have been a relative of Cyrus—finally restored order in 522. Darius, who ruled for more than 30 years, focused initially on reestablishing Cyrus's empire. Once this was accomplished, he proceeded to introduce a remarkable system of imperial administration. He divided the empire into 20 provinces and selected a loyal Persian official—known as a **satrap**—to head each one. He also drew up a new legal code for the empire, developed an extensive and well-protected road system, began minting gold and silver coins, and created a professional army. (Darius himself was protected by a force of 10,000 bodyguards, known as "the Immortals.") In 512 BCE, Darius started construction of a grand complex of buildings in Persepolis, including palaces, treasuries, and banquet halls. The ruins of Darius's imperial city remain one of Iran's most impressive sites.

Darius expanded the Persian Empire east as far as India, and north as far as the Danube River in Europe. It is estimated that, at the height of his empire, Darius ruled over 50 million people. But by 490 BCE, several Greek colonies that were under Persian rule rebelled, encouraged by Sparta and Athens, the two most powerful Greek **city-states**. Darius sent a force to put down the rebellions, but the Athenians defeated his troops at the Battle of Marathon. Soon, Egypt also rebelled against Persian rule. Darius died in 486 BCE, leaving his son Xerxes the task of preserving the empire.

CONFLICTS WITH THE GREEKS

Initially, Xerxes appeared to be succeeding in holding and even expanding his father's empire. In 480 BCE, he attacked Greece, overcoming the Spartan army at the Battle of Thermopylae and then sacking Athens. But the Athenians retaliated by decimating the Persian fleet at the Battle of Salamis, one of history's most famous naval battles. The Persians never fully recovered from this defeat, and in 479 they were driven out of Greece. Xerxes was assassinated in a palace **coup** in 465, and there followed a succession of weak and ineffective rulers.

In 338 BCE Philip, king of Macedon, completed his conquest of the Greek city-states, creating the first unified Greek nation. Upon Philip's death in 336, his son, Alexander the Great, sought to destroy the Persian Empire once and for all. By 331 he had largely succeeded, having defeated Persian armies in three major battles and invaded the Plateau of Iran. Alexander looted the Persian treasury at Susa and razed the palace complex in Persepolis. The Persian Achaemenid Empire came to an end.

Alexander the Great continued his westward march, eventually expanding his empire as far as India. When he died in 323 BCE, Alexander's vast empire was divided among four of his generals, one of whom, Seleucas, became ruler of Iran. Subsequent Greek rulers of Iran, known as the Seleucids, attempted to integrate Greek and Persian culture. But the Seleucids never secured a firm hold on Iran, in part because of pressure from the Ptolemies (the Greek dynasty that ruled Egypt) and the growing power of the Romans.

Another threat to the Seleucids came from the Parthians, a trib-

This statue of Shapur I, the Sasanian king who in 260 CE won a decisive victory over the Roman Empire, stands in a cave in Bishapur, Iran. It is nearly 20 feet (6 meters) tall.

al people from northeastern Iran and the Caspian Sea area. As the Parthians grew increasingly powerful, Seleucid control over Iran weakened. By 140 BCE, the Parthians, under their great leader Mithridates, had effectively ended Seleucid rule and gained control of most of Iran. But in the process, the Parthians drew the attention of the Romans, who feared their growing power. For more than 200 years—from 53 BCE until 218 CE—the Parthians and Romans fought a series of inconclusive and costly wars.

THE SASANIAN EMPIRE (224–642 CE)

Constant warfare with Rome so weakened the Parthians that by 224 CE their empire came under internal attack from the Sasanians, a Persian clan. By 240 the Sasanians had secured control of Iran and much of the former territory of the Achaemenids. In 260 the Sasanian king Shapur I led his armies to a great victory over the Romans; the two empires continued to battle on and off for the next three centuries.

The Sasanians developed a centralized system of government that was based on glorification of the king, who was known as "the king of kings, partner of the stars, brother of the sun and moon." After their deaths, Sasanian kings were worshiped as **deities**. The Sasanians also undertook elaborate irrigation projects that greatly increased agricultural production. They also established a number of new cities. Sasanian kings closely aligned themselves with the Zoroastrian religion, which under their rule became in effect the official religion of Iran. As a result, Zoroastrian priests amassed great power and authority, sometimes rivaling that of the king.

By the late sixth century, the Sasanian Empire was in decline. The wars against the Roman Empire (and later, the Byzantine, or Eastern Roman, Empire) had depleted the treasury, exhausted the military, and generated internal dissension. The weakened state of the empire made it ripe for invasion from abroad.

THE ISLAMIC INVASION

The prophet Muhammad, an Arab merchant from what is today Saudi Arabia, founded the Islamic religion based on revelations he said he received from God. Muhammad and his followers rapidly gained control of the Arabian Peninsula. After his death in 632, his followers—called Muslims—stormed out of Arabia to spread Islam's message throughout the world.

In 635 Muhammad's successor, Abu Bakr, defeated the Byzantine army in Syria and turned his attention to Iran and the crumbling Sasanian Empire. In a series of decisive battles between 637 and 642, the Muslim forces routed the Sasanians. By the year 700, Iran was under the control of the Muslim **caliph** of Damascus, although many parts of the country remained in the hands of former Sasanian governors, who simply paid tribute to the caliph.

The Iranian people were relatively quick to convert to Islam, and in the face of the Arabs' military victories the Zoroastrian priests were unable to put up much resistance. Islam was tolerant of other religions but required non-Muslims to pay high taxes to the caliph. This encouraged widespread conversion by all except the most devout Zoroastrians, many of whom migrated to India, where they became known as Parsis. The Muslim victors allowed converts to keep their land, another inducement to adopting the new religion. But Islam also gained ground among the people of Iran because of its straightforward and egalitarian message: "There is but one God, Allah, and his prophet is Muhammad." Anyone who professed this message and agreed to practice the other four "pillars" of Islam was accepted as a good Muslim, regardless of his or her standing in life, tribal origins, or previous religious beliefs.

The Damascus caliphate—known as the Umayyad—was overthrown in 750 by a rival group, the Abbasids, who moved the capital of the caliphate to Baghdad. Like the Umayyads, the

Abbasids were Arabs, but during their dynasty the influence of Iranians within the caliphate grew. This was especially true in the military and among many of the top court advisers to the caliph. The caliph Mamoun, who came to power in 811, reportedly had an Iranian mother. Their growing influence in the caliphate helped to make Iranians more accepted within the Islamic world. In addition, new commercial ties with the Arabian Peninsula and the rest of the Muslim world benefited Iranians, who prospered economically under both the Umayyads and the Abbasids.

By the ninth century, Abbasid power had begun to weaken. The Abbasid caliphs became virtual figureheads, while real power rested in the hands of local warlords and tribal leaders. Increasingly, Iran came under the influence of Turkish tribes, most of which had also converted to Islam. The most important of these were the Seljuk Turks, who moved south and west into Iran at the beginning of the 11th century. In 1050 the Abbasid caliph in Baghdad anointed the Seljuk leader, Tughril Beg, as "King of the East," acknowledging his control over Iran. During the Seljuks' rule, Iranian culture flourished. The Turkish dynasty encouraged new developments in art, literature, and science, and built religious schools in the major towns and cities. Omar Khayyám, a mathematician and

The Mongol ruler Genghis Khan, at the head of an army of more than 100,000 fierce horsemen, swept into the Plateau of Iran in the 13th century and laid waste to many of the area's cities. Mongol rule in Iran lasted until 1335.

poet, and Abou Hamed Ghazzali, one of Islam's most important theologians, were among the great scholars who lived and thrived in Seljuk Iran.

INVADERS FROM CENTRAL ASIA

In 1219 the Mongol warrior Genghis Khan and his army of perhaps 120,000 stormed across the Plateau of Iran, burning and looting cities along the way. Unlike the Arab invaders, who brought a new religion to Iran and encouraged the arts and literature, the Mongols were bent on destruction. The gained control of all of Iran, and in 1258 Mongol warriors captured Baghdad and killed the last Abbasid caliph. At its greatest extent, the Mongol Empire stretched from China to Turkey. The descendants of Genghis Khan ruled Iran until 1335, when the last Mongol ruler died without a successor.

After several decades of fragmented rule by regional warlords, Iran was once again invaded from outside, this time by Tamerlane, a Turkic leader. Tamerlane swept out of central Asia to capture most of Iran as well as parts of Turkey and India. But Tamerlane established no solid structures of government, and when he died in

Caravans traveling the deserts of Iran once stopped at this complex for rest and shelter. Constructed during the reign of the Safavid shah Abbas I (1587–1629), it is located near Isfahan.

1405 his empire quickly disintegrated. Iran once again experienced fragmentation and decline.

THE SAFAVID EMPIRE (1501–1722)

In 1501 Iran came under the control of a group of militant religious leaders known as the Safavids; their leader, Ismael, proclaimed himself shah of Iran. The Safavids were Sufis, an order of religious mystics, and adherents to the Shia sect of Islam. When the prophet Muhammad died in 632, he left no appointed successor. A rift immediately developed between those who favored Muhammad's son-in-law, Ali, and those who favored Muhammad's closest companion, Abu Bakr. The followers of Ali became known as the Shia (from the expression "Shi'at Ali," which means "partisan of Ali"). Those who backed Abu Bakr were known as the Sunni. Over the centuries, Sunnism became the dominant—or "orthodox"—sect of Islam, while members of the Shia branch remained a minority. Upon coming to power, the Safavids immediately declared Shia Islam the state religion of Iran, and Iran has been the world's largest and most important Shia nation ever since.

The greatest Safavid was Shah Abbas I, who ruled from 1587 until 1629. Shah Abbas successfully waged war against the Turkish Ottoman Empire, which had been threatening western Iran. He moved his capital to Isfahan, which he adorned with magnificent architectural monuments, mosques, and palaces. He welcomed European traders to Iran and encouraged Iranians to develop thriving industries in silk, carpet weaving, and metalwork. Shah Abbas was also a patron of the arts, which flourished under his rule.

Following Shah Abbas's death, Iran once again descended into fragmentation and disorder. Subsequent Safavid rulers were weak, and the heavy taxation required to maintain the armed forces led to resentment and rebellions. In 1722 the weakened Safavid Empire was toppled by invading Afghans, who seized Isfahan. In

1727 a general named Nader Khan grabbed control and, for the next 20 years, used Iran as a base for military exploits. Although he was successful on the battlefield—looting cities as far east as India and fending off the Ottomans and Russians in the west—Nader Khan failed to establish a lasting dynasty.

THE QAJARS (1795–1925)

Another power struggle among rival tribal clans took place after Nader Khan's death, and ultimately the Qajars seized control. The Qajar leaders gradually secured power throughout the country by appointing loyal provincial governors. The Shia religious leaders, however, maintained a large degree of autonomy.

At the beginning of the 19th century, Iran became the focus of attention of two European powers, Russia and Britain. Both countries had imperial interests they wanted to protect, and both recognized Iran's strategic importance. The British were concerned primarily with protecting their trade routes to India, the most important British colony. Russia was interested in expanding southward so as to gain access to the warm waters of the Persian Gulf and Indian Ocean.

The Qajars fought two wars with Russia—in 1812 and 1828—both of which the Iranians lost, leading to Russian territorial gains in the Caucasus Mountains and central Asia. Britain moved troops into eastern Iran to prevent the Qajars from advancing toward Afghanistan. In 1857 the Qajars ceded to Britain all claims to Afghanistan.

These setbacks at the hands of foreign powers caused a growing number of Iranians to begin encouraging the Qajar rulers to modernize the country along the lines of European nations. Otherwise, they argued, Iran would never be able to compete with and fend off the European imperial powers. These reformers met resistance from religious leaders, who favored keeping Iran isolated from the "corrupting" influences of Europe and who feared a reduction in their own power. The reformers won a major victory in 1906 when popular unrest against foreign influence forced the Qajar shah to institute an elected parliament—known as the **Majlis**—and a constitution that, for the first time in Iran's long history, placed limits on the shah's power.

The reformers, however, were unable to preserve their achievements. In 1908, with Russian assistance, the shah bombed the Majlis building and disbanded the parliament. Reformist forces drove the shah from power, but he returned in 1910 with more Russian troops, and in 1911 the Majlis was shut down again.

To make matters worse, during this chaotic period the Russians and British signed an agreement, in 1907, that essentially divided Iran between them: Russia would have influence in the north, Britain in the south and east. During World War I (1914–18), Germany attempted to disrupt British control over Iran by supporting tribal uprisings in the south. Russia, meanwhile, preoccupied by its own Bolshevik (Communist) revolution, withdrew from Iran, leaving a power vacuum in the north. After World War I ended, Britain used financial inducements to persuade the shah to sign the Anglo-Persian Agreement of 1919, which made Iran a virtual British **protectorate**. The agreement, however, aroused great opposition among Iranians.

THE PAHLAVIS (1925–1979)

In 1921 a military officer named Reza Khan marched into Tehran and seized control of the government, forcing the shah to appoint him defense minister and then prime minister. In 1925 Reza Khan persuaded the Majlis to abolish the Qajar dynasty; he was coronated as Reza Shah Pahlavi. The new shah believed that Iran had not kept pace with the European powers and needed to modernize quickly. He began by creating a disciplined, European-style army to maintain his control. He improved the administration of government, built **secular** schools throughout the country (up to this point, most education in Iran had been through religious schools), and established the country's first university, in Tehran. He also pushed through other measures to limit the power and influence of the religious leaders (for example, by replacing religious courts of law with secular courts) and the feudal landlords (by confiscating and redistributing their lands).

In the economic realm, the shah expanded the road network, completed the first railroad to traverse the entire country, and built government-owned factories to provide basic necessities and employment opportunities. He imposed European-style dress on the Iranian people and ordered that women were no longer to wear the veil, a traditional Islamic custom that he viewed as archaic.

But the shah ruled with an iron fist. The Majlis ultimately became powerless. Political opponents and journalists were jailed—or worse, executed without trial. The shah established a secret police that rounded up religious leaders who opposed his social reforms. Public protests were dealt with harshly.

In foreign affairs, the shah sought to limit the influence of

Reza Shah Pahlavi, seen here in a 1931 photo, promoted rapid modernization in Iran but ruled with an iron fist. A former army officer named Reza Khan, he had himself crowned shah after ousting the Qajar dynasty.

Britain and the Soviet Union (which had been formed in 1922, following the victory of the Bolsheviks in Russia). He was particularly eager to revoke agreements that had given British companies a monopoly over Iran's oil production and resources. He also encouraged Germany to establish a greater economic and political presence in Iran as a counterweight to the British and Soviets.

When World War II broke out, the shah declared Iran neutral, greatly angering both the British and the Soviets, who used his overtures toward Germany as an excuse to invade Iran in 1941. With Soviet forces marching southward from the Caucasus Mountains and British troops invading from the west and south, Shah Reza Pahlavi fled the country for South Africa, where he died in exile in 1944.

The shah was succeeded by his 22-year-old son, Mohammed Reza Pahlavi, who proved to be much more cooperative with the British and Russians. In 1942 the young shah signed an agreement that exchanged Iran's support in the war effort for a pledge by the two great powers to withdraw their troops after the war was over and to acknowledge Iran's sovereignty and independence. In 1943 the United States, which also had deployed troops to Iran, joined in this pledge when President Franklin D. Roosevelt met in Tehran with the shah, Soviet leader Joseph Stalin, and British prime minister Winston Churchill.

After the war, the British and Americans withdrew their forces from Iran as promised. But the Soviets stalled. They attempted to meddle in Iranian affairs in collusion with the anti-shah Iranian Communist Party (known as the Tudeh Party) and with Kurdish nationalists in the northwest. It took pressure from the United States, Britain, and the United Nations before the Soviets finally withdrew their troops from the country. In 1947 the United States and Iran signed an agreement pledging military and economic cooperation, and in 1949 the shah banned the pro-Soviet Tudeh Party.

Since 1909 Iran's oil production had been controlled by a British firm, the Anglo-Iranian Oil Company, or AIOC (initially it was known as the Anglo-Persian Oil Company, or APOC). Under this arrangement, most of the profits went to the British. Around 1950 public sentiment in Iran began to grow in favor of **nationalization**; Iranians wanted more control over their oil resources and the profits these resources produced. In 1951 the Majlis voted to nationalize the oil industry. Although the shah favored an amicable agreement with the AIOC, he relented to the Majlis's pressure and appointed a fierce nationalist, Mohammed Mossadeq, as prime minister.

The British retaliated by withdrawing all AIOC engineers and technicians from Iran, causing oil production to grind to a halt. Iranians were initially behind Mossadeq, but as the economy faltered from the loss of oil revenues, the political situation became volatile. In 1953 Mossadeq dissolved the Majlis and appeared headed toward authoritarian control, displacing the pro-Western shah. Fearful that Mossadeq was in cahoots with Communists, the United States and Britain undertook a secret operation—spearheaded by the U.S. Central Intelligence Agency (CIA)—to have him overthrown. The shah regained his power with strong backing from the United States and Britain.

The shah felt that the greatest threat to Iran came from the Soviet Union, so in 1955 he joined a military alliance with the United States and accepted large-scale U.S. military and economic assistance. The shah also clamped down on Communists and other supporters of Mossadeq.

In 1963 the shah launched a new economic reform and modernization program, dubbed the "White Revolution." The program included a new emphasis on education and literacy, and the more equal sharing of landholdings. These measures greatly angered the clergy, as did the shah's close relations with Israel and a "Status of Forces Agreement" that made American military personnel exempt from Iranian laws. One of these religious leaders, Ayatollah Ruhollah Khomeini, began to preach against the shah and his reforms. Khomeini was arrested and exiled to Turkey in 1964.

Over the next decade, the shah continued to implement reform and modernization programs, but he also strengthened his personal power and that of the monarchy. In 1971 the shah held a lavish and expensive celebration at Persepolis in commemoration of the 2,500th anniversary of the founding of the first Persian empire under Cyrus the Great. The real purpose of the celebration, however, was to link the Pahlavi monarchy to Persia's glorious imperial past and to solidify the shah's own position as the undisputed leader of Iran. From exile, Ayatollah Khomeini condemned the celebration and the growing power of the shah.

Iran's economy prospered in the early 1970s, and combined with its growing military arsenal, this allowed the country to begin playing a dominant role in regional affairs. Iran maintained close ties with the other major U.S. allies in the region, such as Saudi Arabia and the United Arab Emirates. The shah believed that Iran's destiny was to be the "guardian" of the Persian Gulf region, and U.S. president Richard Nixon encouraged him along this path. During his 1972 visit to Iran, Nixon promised to sell to Iran any conventional (non-nuclear) weaponry the shah desired. In exchange, the shah allowed the United States to set up radar "listening posts" in northern Iran to monitor the Soviet Union.

But while the shah's stature rose on the international stage, opposition to his authoritarian rule at home continued to grow. Throughout the early 1970s, Ayatollah Khomeini issued a steady stream of denunciations of the shah's policies and secretly established a network of supporters within Iran. Khomeini said that a monarchy such as that of the Pahlavis was contradictory to Islamic principles; he called for the establishment of an Islamic state, governed solely by religious guidelines. Many international human rights groups also started to criticize the shah for suppressing opposition and preventing freedom of the press.

THE ISLAMIC REVOLUTION

By the late 1970s, Iran's economic boom had fizzled out. The shah had spent so much of the country's oil wealth on weapons and expensive construction projects that there was very little left for social programs. The effect was to broaden opposition to the shah beyond merely the religious establishment. In the cities the working classes, civil servants, and students increasingly began to protest against the shah. In 1978 these protests turned violent and spread rapidly to virtually all of Iran's major cities. The protests also took on a religious nature and were often led by Islamic clerics who were followers of Khomeini. From exile, Khomeini openly called for the overthrow of the shah and his government.

The shah attempted to calm the protests by releasing **political prisoners** and announcing new rules allowing greater freedom of speech. In response to his devout religious critics, the shah closed casinos and nightclubs. But it was too late to stem the tide of opposition. After the shah's police fired on protesters in Tehran on September 7, 1978—killing dozens—factory workers, students, and government bureaucrats went on strike, refusing to work and gathering in Iran's cities for huge demonstrations and clashes with the police.

On January 16, 1979, the shah announced that he was leaving the country for a short vacation. As it turned out, he would never return to Iran. On February 1, 1979, after 11 years in exile, Ayatollah Khomeini arrived at Tehran Airport to a tumultuous welcome. Khomeini immediately appointed a provisional government, but large parts of the country remained in a state of chaos and uncertainty. Local supporters of Khomeini—known as "Revolutionary Committees"—were often the only authority in many urban neighbor-

Iranians stand in front of a huge poster of Ayatollah Ruhollah Khomeini, the spiritual leader of the 1979 Islamic Revolution, which overthrew the shah.

hoods. Many people feared that the Iranian army would resist Khomeini's takeover of the government and attempt a coup. In fact, military leaders soon announced that they would not fight against Khomeini's supporters. On April 1, 1979, Khomeini proclaimed that henceforth the country would be known as the Islamic Republic of Iran. Khomeini himself was named the Supreme Leader, with the authority to determine the direction of the revolution.

Although Khomeini appointed a prime minister, real power rested in the hands of the Revolutionary Council, led by Khomeini and composed of Shia religious leaders who supported him. Under directions from the Revolutionary Council, a system of Revolutionary Courts was set up to arrest and try former members of the shah's government. More than 500 were executed for "crimes against the people." Khomeini also established the Islamic Revolution Guards Corps (often referred to simply as the Revolutionary Guards), an armed force intended to defend the revolution against internal threats. The Revolutionary Council imposed a series of economic rulings that led to the nationalization of many factories and businesses and the ***expropriation*** of private property and wealth. The Revolutionary Committees continued to control the cities. Eventually, the prime minister resigned, acknowledging that he had lost authority and that the Revolutionary Council in fact controlled the country.

A major focus of Khomeini's revolution was transforming Iranian society so that it better reflected Islamic values. The country's new leaders made Islamic studies a major part of the school curriculum, replaced the existing judicial system with one based on Islamic law, and established anti-vice squads to ensure that Islamic customs and laws were obeyed. The most significant changes concerned the role and status of women. Khomeini's government imposed laws that required women to cover themselves with a veil (known as *hejab*) when in public and kept women separated from men in schools and workplaces.

THE HOSTAGE CRISIS

In October 1979 the U.S. government allowed the former shah, who had been living in exile in Egypt, to enter the United States for medical treatment for cancer. But many Iranians saw this as an American attempt to bolster the shah, perhaps as a prelude to a U.S.–led effort to overthrow the Islamic Republic. On November 1, 1979, hundreds of thousands of Iranians protested in the streets against the United States. Three days later, a gang of Iranian students stormed the U.S. embassy building and took more than 60 American diplomats and embassy staffers hostage. Although the action appeared to be spontaneous, Khomeini himself praised the hostage-takers and refused to call for the release of the hostages. U.S. president Jimmy Carter froze all Iranian financial assets in the United States and imposed other economic **sanctions** on Iran.

The hostage crisis further intensified the struggle within Iran between those who wanted to establish a stable and effective government and those who preferred to continue the revolution. In

President Jimmy Carter signs a document demanding the release of the American hostages seized at the U.S. embassy in Tehran in November 1979. The hostage crisis, which dragged on until January 1981, poisoned U.S.-Iranian relations.

January 1980, Iranians elected a new president (from a list of candidates approved by Khomeini): Abolhassan Bani-Sadr. Bani-Sadr attempted to create a centralized government and to weaken the power of the religious leaders. But the Revolutionary Guards and Revolutionary Committees maintained the upper hand. Against Bani-Sadr's wishes, hundreds of Iranian military officers, accused of loyalty to the shah, were executed.

In April 1980 President Carter ordered a military operation to rescue the hostages, but the mission had to be aborted when U.S. helicopters developed mechanical problems. Later, during a sandstorm, a helicopter and a transport plane collided in the Iranian desert, killing eight American soldiers. In September 1980, Iran and the United States began to negotiate over the release of the hostages. Carter, who was in a tight reelection race against former California governor Ronald Reagan, hoped to have the hostages home before the election in November. But Iran drew out the negotiations past November, and Carter lost the election. On January 20, 1981—the day Ronald Reagan was inaugurated president—Iran freed the remaining 52 American hostages (about a dozen had been released earlier) after 444 days in captivity. U.S.-Iranian relations, however, remained very bad, with virtually no official contact between the two countries' governments.

WAR WITH IRAQ

In September 1980, ongoing tensions along Iran's border with Iraq erupted into full-fledged warfare. Iraq, a country fractured along religious and ethnic lines, had been wary of the Islamic Republic from the first day. Iraq had a majority Shia Muslim population, but power was held by the Sunni minority through the Baath Party and its ruthless leader, Saddam Hussein. Saddam favored a secular government and wanted to modernize his country. He feared that Khomeini's revolutionary message would spread to Iraq's Shia community and that Iran was in fact trying to instigate his overthrow. In addition, Iran and Iraq had long-running disagreements over the demarcation of their border. In 1975 Iraq and Iran had reached an understanding on this issue, called the Algiers Accord, but Saddam now feared that the Islamic Republic would repudiate the agreement. Another factor leading to war was Saddam's accurate assessment that Iran was in a state of near turmoil, with dissension among the military (many of whose officers had been executed). Saddam believed that this was the time to attack his much larger neighbor and grab control of some of Iran's oil-rich regions. Although officially neutral, the United States tacitly supported Saddam's invasion and provided the Iraqis with intelligence information throughout the war.

The Iran-Iraq War devastated both countries. It is estimated that more than 1 million people on both sides were killed or wounded in the fighting, and millions of Iranians were forced to flee their homes. The economic cost of the war was staggering as well. As the fighting dragged on without a clear victor, Iraq began to target Iranian oil facilities and to attack Iranian cities with long-range missiles. Iran retaliated by attacking oil tankers in the Persian Gulf.

President Reagan sent the U.S. Navy to protect these tankers (many of which transported oil destined for the United States). This led to several clashes between U.S. and Iranian forces. In one tragic incident, a U.S. naval ship, the *Vincennes*, shot down an Iranian passenger jet, which it mistook for a military aircraft. All 290 people aboard were killed.

Although President Reagan apologized, the 1988 *Vincennes* incident further soured relations between the United States and Iran. But it seems also to have helped end the Iran-Iraq War. The Iranian regime was never persuaded that the *Vincennes* incident was an accident, and their interpretation of it as a sign of a strengthened U.S. commitment to prevent Iran from winning the war helped lead to a U.N.-sponsored cease-fire later that year.

Because it gave them an external enemy to motivate their followers, the war helped the revolutionary elements in Iranian society strengthen their control. Those who wished to limit the power of the religious leaders rapidly lost support in the first years of the fighting. In July 1981 President Bani-Sadr was impeached by the religious-controlled Majlis—and forced to flee for his life. His successor, who was handpicked by Khomeini, was assassinated in a bombing carried out by forces opposed to the religious leadership.

Hit by an Iranian rocket, an oil tanker burns in the Persian Gulf during the Iran-Iraq War. The eight-year conflict devastated both countries.

This provided Khomeini and his followers with an excuse to clamp down on dissenters, and by the end of 1982 Khomeini had effectively suppressed all opposition.

IRAN AFTER KHOMEINI

Khomeini died in June 1989. Millions of Iranians packed the streets of Tehran for his funeral procession. A small group of religious leaders, known as the Assembly of Experts, met secretly to appoint the Ayatollah Ali Khamenei to be Khomeini's successor as Supreme Leader. In July, **Hojatoleslam** Ali Akbar Hashemi Rafsanjani was elected president.

Rafsanjani continued many of the revolutionary policies of Khomeini, including strong opposition to the United States. Iran condemned Iraq's 1990 invasion of Kuwait, but it also opposed the U.S.-led coalition that drove Saddam's forces out of Kuwait and took a public stance of neutrality. Soon after Rafsanjani was reelected president in 1993, U.S. president Bill Clinton imposed strict economic sanctions on Iran, banning virtually all U.S. trade with the Islamic Republic. Clinton accused Iran of supporting international terrorism, of attempting to develop nuclear weapons, and of opposing the U.S. effort to bring about a negotiated peace between Israel and the Palestinians.

At home, Rafsanjani focused on rebuilding Iran's war-shattered economy. He also attempted to ease Iran's isolation by pushing for laws to encourage foreign investment and trade. Falling international oil prices, however, reduced Iran's income and forced the government to reduce spending on many social services. This resulted in a lower standard of living for average citizens, many of whom responded by protesting in the streets.

In the 1997 presidential elections, Iranians stunned the world by electing Hojatoleslam Mohammed Khatami, a relatively progressive candidate who was clearly not the favored choice of the religious leadership. Although himself a cleric and Islamic scholar, Khatami was an advocate of greater personal liberties and press freedom, and during the campaign he suggested that the religious leadership had become too powerful.

Khatami's election gave new confidence to reformist forces in Iran and to those who wanted to restrict the power of the religious leaders. In elections for parliament in February 2000, reformist candidates won 70 percent of the seats, with only 14 percent of the seats going to Islamic clerics. (By contrast, in the 1980 elections more than 50 percent of the seats were won by Islamic clerics.) In an effort to end Iran's international isolation, Khatami proposed that the United States and Iran take steps to "break the walls of mistrust" between the two nations.

Conservative religious forces in Iran strongly resisted Khatami's policies, however. Iranian courts still under the control of the religious leadership shut down a number of newspapers and journals that advocated a more progressive direction for the country. Students and other pro-reform Iranians responded with vocal demonstrations demanding greater freedoms. In June 2001 Khatami won reelection in a landslide, a clear signal that the Iranian people favored his progressive and reformist policies. But the Islamic leadership still held considerable power, through Supreme Leader Ayatollah Ali Khamenei, the senate-like Council of Guardians, and other unelected bodies.

The tension between reformers and hard-liners was evident in the aftermath of the September 11, 2001, al-Qaeda terrorist attacks against New York and Washington, D.C. In an interview, Khatami called the attacks "horrific," and he strongly condemned terrorist chief Osama bin Laden. But just six days later, Supreme Leader Khamenei said on Iranian television, "America's expansionist policies were the cause of recent developments."

For his part, U.S. president George W. Bush took a bellicose stance toward Iran. In his 2002 State of the Union Address, Bush said the Islamic Republic was seeking to develop weapons of mass destruction (chemical, biological, and nuclear weapons) and that it exported terrorism. Bush further said that Iran, along with Iraq and North Korea, constituted an "axis of evil."

By the end of 2002, Iran—with technical assistance from Russia—began reconstructing a nuclear reactor near Bushehr, which had been extensively damaged during the Iran-Iraq War. The move contributed to international concerns that Iran was, in fact, intent on developing nuclear weapons.

In June 2003, student protests against Iran's powerful Shia clerics rocked Tehran. In the ensuing months, however, reformers found themselves outmaneuvered and marginalized by hard-liners. The Council of Guardians disqualified thousands of reform candidates for the Majlis, leaving conservatives in control of the Iranian parliament after the February 2004 elections. The following year, the extremely conservative former mayor of Tehran, Mahmoud Ahmadinejad, was elected president of Iran.

Ahmadinejad quickly gained a reputation for stoking controversy. In October 2005, Western news organizations reported his call that Israel "must be wiped off the map"—although some scholars questioned the accuracy of the translation. Ahmadinejad's confrontational foreign policy had consequences that were not always welcomed at home. For instance, in April 2007 Ahmadinejad announced that Iran was capable of producing large quantities of nuclear fuel. The International Atomic Energy Agency estimated that Iran would be able to develop an atomic bomb in as little as three years. Anticipating international trade and economic sanctions because of its nuclear program, the Iranian government began rationing gasoline, touching off large protests in Iran.

In recent years, much of the attention given Iran by the rest of the world has focused on its nuclear development. Many leaders, especially in western nations, fear the prospect of Iran acquiring a nuclear arsenal. The Iranian government insists it is developing nuclear power only for peaceful purposes.

The Iranian government also has been accused of supporting international terrorism by Islamic jihadists. Although Sunni jihadists theologically oppose Iran's Shiite majority, they share a common hatred of western influences and, particularly, of the existence of Israel.

Ahmadinejad was reelected in 2009—prompting violent protests from reformist citizens who claimed the election was rigged. In 2013, Hassan Rouhani, a reformist cleric, was elected president of Iran.

Hassan Rouhani was elected president of Iran in 2013.

After a long series of negotiations with six world powers, a tentative agreement was announced in April 2015 that would limit Iran's nuclear program. However, many international leaders and political analysts remained leery of Iran's nuclear intentions and its willingness to have its military sites inspected by U.N. officials.

 ## Text-Dependent Questions

1. Who was king of Persia during its grandest period in history?
2. Who were "the Immortals"?
3. In what famous naval battle was the Persian fleet destroyed?

 ## Research Project

Research the history and romance of the Silk Road. Write a report to present to the class.

This oil refinery near Abadan is one of the largest operated by Iran's national oil company, NIORDC. Iran exports around 1.5 million barrels of crude oil a day, making it the second-largest exporter among the Organization of Petroleum Exporting Countries (OPEC).

Politics, the Economy, and Religion

Several enduring factors have shaped Iran's politics over the centuries. For most of the country's long and eventful history, its rulers have been emperors and kings. This established a strong legacy of authoritarian government, in which one supreme ruler, assisted by a circle of advisers and supporters, made the laws and determined the nation's course. Until very recent times, the Iranian people have rarely had the power to elect their leadership or even openly debate the direction the country should take. Even today, when the people have the right to vote, Iran does not resemble a democracy in the American or European sense.

Another important factor shaping Iranian politics is the traumatic history of foreign invasion and attack. Whether it was other empires, such as that of Alexander the Great; marauding tribes, like the Mongols; or conspiring great powers, such as Britain and Russia, foreigners frequently coveted Iran's strategic location and resources. Although the United States has never invaded or directly attacked Iran, in recent years many Iranians have seen it as a hostile foreign power.

At the same time, Iran's own history of regional influence and domination—beginning with the powerful empire of Cyrus the Great—has infused Iranian politics with a sense of destiny and greatness. Iranians are a very proud people. Whoever their leaders have been, all have shared a vision of Iran's preeminent role in the Persian Gulf area as well as the broader Middle East and the Islamic world.

A final enduring factor in Iranian politics has been the ongoing struggle between secular and religious leaders. Sasanian rulers (224 to 642 CE) had to contend with the power and influence of Zoroastrian priests. After the Arab invasion in the seventh century and the country's subsequent conversion to Islam, the clergy has played a dominant role in society. In the 20th century, the struggle between the religious and secular leaderships became highly contentious. Under the Pahlavis, those who wanted to modernize Iran began to see Islamic leaders—and many aspects of the religious tradition they espoused—as a hindrance to the country's political and economic development. With the Islamic Revolution of 1979, the Islamic forces appeared to win the struggle. But 30 years later, Iranians once again are wrestling with their nation's future,

Words to Understand in This Chapter

bazaar—a large market, often covered, containing hundreds of shops.
cartel—a group of countries that trade a common resource (such as oil) and join together to set the price of that resource.
foreign exchange—money earned by trading goods or services with other countries.
infrastructure—the basic economic assets of a country, such as roads, electric power plants, and so on.
Qur'an—the Muslim holy book.

Islamic motifs dominate the flag of Iran. In the center is a stylized representation of the word *Allah* ("God") in the shape of a tulip, which is a symbol of martyrdom. The words *Allahu akbar* ("God is great") are repeated in stylized Arabic along the bottom edge of the green band and the top edge of the red band.

attempting to reconcile religious tradition with democracy and modernization.

Politics in the Islamic Republic of Iran

In April 1979 the Ayatollah Khomeini declared that henceforth the country would be known as the Islamic Republic of Iran. The era of kings and dynasties appeared to be over, but it was unclear how a new system of government would be structured or how much power the average citizen would have in selecting Iran's leaders. In October 1979 the leaders of the revolution drafted a new constitution, which declared that the role of government in the new Islamic Republic would be "to establish an ideal and model society on the basis of Islamic norms." The constitution included numerous passages from the Holy **Qur'an** (often spelled Koran), Islam's sacred book, but it also contained elements of a modern democracy. It outlined a very complex system of government with overlapping authority and significant control by religious leaders. The constitution was

Ayatollah Khomeini spent 15 years in exile before returning to Iran in 1979. As "Supreme Leader," he used his near-absolute power to transform Iranian politics and society along the lines of conservative Shia Islam—and he tried to export this "Islamic Revolution" to other countries.

ratified in a nationwide referendum in December 1979.

The most important position in the Islamic Republic, as established by the constitution, is that of Supreme Leader. The Supreme Leader is supposed to be a senior religious figure and is not elected by the people. The constitution also established a president and parliament, both elected by the people, and a judicial system based on Islamic law. In addition, several appointed councils were established to ensure the Islamic direction of the country.

THE SUPREME LEADER

According to Iran's constitution, the Supreme Leader is the single most powerful political figure in Iran. He is charged with establishing the general direction of Iran's domestic and foreign policies, serves as commander-in-chief of the armed forces and intelligence services, and can appoint and dismiss judges and the heads of the state-controlled radio and television networks. He appoints 6 of the 12 members of the powerful Council of Guardians and officially ratifies the president's election. The Supreme Leader serves for life.

Ayatollah Khomeini, Iran's first Supreme Leader, held the position until his death in 1989. He was succeeded by another senior religious figure, Ayatollah Sayyid Ali Khamenei, who remained the Supreme Leader as of 2015.

The Supreme Leader is selected by—and in theory, may be dismissed by—the Assembly of Experts, which consists of 86 Islamic clerics. The Assembly is supposed to meet twice each year to assess the performance of the Supreme Leader. Members are elected by the Iranian people for eight-year terms (the next election is scheduled in February 2016), giving the impression that the Assembly is a democratically elected body. But in fact, the Council of Guardians determines who among the country's many Islamic clerics may run for the Assembly of Experts, and the Assembly's deliberations are never made public.

THE COUNCIL OF GUARDIANS

The secretive Council of Guardians is perhaps the most important institution in Iran. It consists of 12 members: six clerics who are appointed by the Supreme Leader and six legal scholars who are appointed by the country's senior judicial official, who also is appointed by the Supreme Leader. The Council has the power to determine who may run for any elective office—the presidency, the parliament, or the Assembly of Experts. It bases its decision on whether or not the prospective candidate is sufficiently committed to the goals of the Islamic Revolution. The Council has a record of prohibiting prospective candidates whose views may not be closely in line with those of the strict Islamic government.

In addition, the Council of Guardians has the power to approve or reject any legislation passed by the parliament. If the Council rules that laws passed by the parliament violate Islamic law and principles, it can demand that they be revised or abolished.

THE ISLAMIC REVOLUTION GUARDS CORPS (IRGC)

Established in 1979 to defend the Islamic Revolution against any forces in Iranian society that might wish to stop or hinder it, the Islamic Revolution Guards Corps (IRGC) is, like the armed forces, controlled by the Supreme Leader. The IRGC played a major role in the war with Iraq and emerged from that conflict with even greater power and influence. A militia affiliated with the IRGC, known as the "Basij," has a domestic security function and serves as an internal "army" to defend the interests of the conservative religious leadership.

THE PRESIDENT

Iran's president is directly elected by the people (from a list of candidates approved by the Council of Guardians) for a four-year term; he may serve only two consecutive terms. The president is head of the executive branch, appoints the cabinet (with the approval of the parliament), and is largely responsible for economic policy. However, he does not control the armed forces, nor does he determine the overall direction of Iran's domestic and foreign policies (those powers belong to the Supreme Leader). But as a popularly elected figure, the president has a high public profile. In June 2009, President Mahmoud Ahmadinejad won reelection, despite widespread doubts about the fairness of the voting. Massive protests and a violent government crackdown followed the disputed election. Hassan Rouhani, viewed by outsiders as a moderate in Iranian politics, was elected president in 2013.

THE PARLIAMENT

Iran's 290-member parliament, known as the Majlis, is elected by the people every four years. Like most parliaments in the world, the Majlis drafts legislation, approves the national budget, and ratifies international treaties. But any legislation it passes must be approved by the Council of Guardians before becoming the law of the land. The constitution guarantees that three religious minority groups—Jews, Zoroastrians, and Christians—each have one seat in the Majlis. The first post-revolution Majlis, elected in 1980, was

Iran's parliament, called the Majlis, meets in this chamber. The 290 members of the Majlis are elected by popular vote every four years.

composed mostly of religious scholars and leaders of the revolution. In recent years, the Majlis has included more secular leaders.

THE JUDICIARY

Under Iran's constitution, the country's legal system is based on Islamic law, which derives from scholars' interpretation of the Qur'an. The judiciary branch of government is heavily controlled by the Supreme Leader: he appoints the head of the judiciary, who in turn appoints the head of the Supreme Court and the public prosecutor, as well as six members of the powerful Council of Guardians.

Iran has several court systems. Public courts deal with regular criminal and civil cases. Trials in public courts may be attended by anyone, and verdicts may be appealed all the way up to the Supreme Court. The constitution demands that judges' rulings do not "conflict with the laws or the norms of Islam." "Revolutionary courts" deal with any crimes against national security or crimes that are deemed to undermine the Islamic Republic. The special court for the clergy is supposed to deal with any cases that relate to religious officials.

IRANIAN POLITICS TODAY

Since 1997, Iranian politics has been characterized by tension between religious conservatives, who remain committed to the strict principles of the Islamic Revolution, and reformists, who wish to change aspects of Iran's political system to make it more open and democratic. For the most part, however, the reformists wish to maintain Iran as an Islamic Republic, and some of the most vocal reformers are clerics. The surprising landslide victory of Hojatoleslam Mohammed Khatami in the 1997 presidential election was an indication of the degree to which the Iranian people desired to move away from the most rigid aspects of the Islamic Revolution.

Khatami is a cleric who studied theology at religious schools in the Iranian city of Qom, a major center of Shia religious study. He was close to Ayatollah Khomeini and other leaders of the revolution.

Students at the University of Tehran protest the death sentence handed down against Hashem Aghajari, a professor who was charged with blasphemy for criticizing Iran's Shiite clerics. The outcome of the power struggle between Islamic fundamentalists who wish to continue the legacy of the Ayatollah Khomeini and reformers who advocate a more secular, open society will determine the future direction of Iran.

But he also studied Western philosophy and lived for more than a decade in Germany.

Khatami was one of only four candidates the Council of Guardians approved to run for president. Running on a platform promising greater personal freedoms, and benefiting from his great personal charisma, Khatami garnered a majority of the vote among women and young voters, many of whom were infants during the revolution. He also received the support of many business leaders who wanted to end Iran's isolation from the rest of the world. In the end, Khatami won nearly 70 percent of the vote.

The reformist trend in Iran gained a further boost in the 2000 parliamentary elections, when reformist candidates aligned with Khatami won a majority of seats in the Majlis. But the conservative

Western leaders, as well as many Iranians, hoped that the election of Mohammed Khatami would mark the start of a liberalization of Iranian society. However, the Supreme Leader and Council of Guardians prevented Khatami from implementing meaningful social reforms.

religious forces in Iran held on to several critical bases of power—most importantly, the Supreme Leader, Ayatollah Khamenei, as well as the Council of Guardians, the judiciary, and the IRGC.

A number of reformist newspapers and magazines that supported Khatami's goals were shut down by the authorities, and in some instances security forces and vigilantes assaulted pro-Khatami students and protesters. Government agents assassinated some political dissidents. Other dissidents were jailed.

Frustrated, Khatami considered not running for reelection in 2001, but in the end he entered the race and won by an even greater margin than he had enjoyed in 1997. Once again, his principal sources of support were women and young voters, especially in the larger cities. The reform movement had received another vote of support from the Iranian people, but it still faced a strong and well-organized opposition among the conservative clerics. The internal struggle for power in Iran was escalating.

While the reform movement seemed to be gaining momentum, Iran's political system affords conservative religious forces with important structural advantages, including the broad authority of the Council of Guardians and the Supreme Leader. This was evident in the return of parliament to conservative control in 2004,

 Quick Facts: The Economy of Iran

Gross domestic product (GDP*): $403 billion (rank 164th in the world).
GDP per capita: $16,500 (rank 96th in the world).
GDP growth rate: 1.5% (rank 164th in the world).
Inflation: 17.8%
Unemployment rate: 10.3% (rank 115th in the world).
Natural resources: petroleum, natural gas, coal, iron ore, copper, chromium, manganese, zinc, lead, sulfur.
Agriculture (9.1% of GDP): wheat, rice, sugar beats, fruits, sugarcane, cotton, nuts, wool, dairy products, caviar.
Industry (40.7% of GDP): petroleum, petrochemicals, gas, fertilizers, caustic soda, textiles, food processing, cement and other construction materials, metal fabrication, armaments.
Services (50.3% of GDP): government services (education, health, military, etc.), small enterprises, tourism.
Foreign trade:
  Imports—$61.25 billion: industrial supplies, capital goods, foodstuffs, technical services, various consumer goods.
  Exports—$95.71 billion: petroleum, chemical and petrochemical products, fruits and nuts, carpets, cement, ore.
Currency exchange rate: 25,780.2 Iranian riyals = U.S. $1 (2015)

*GDP, or gross domestic product, is the total value of goods and services produced in a country annually.
All figures are 2014 estimates unless otherwise noted.
Source: CIA World Factbook, 2015.

and the election of hard-liner Mahmoud Ahmadinejad to the presidency the following year. Ahmadinejad was re-elected in 2009—although protests of vote rigging led to violent riots resulting in 30 deaths.

Nevertheless, Iran's population is young—the median age in 2014 was estimated at just 28. In 2013, Iranians elected Hassan Rouhani, a reform-backed cleric, to the presidency. Rouhani has attempted to improve Iran's relations with other countries, including the United States. His administration has also permitted greater freedom for women in Iran, and has appointed several women to high-ranking government positions.

Many Iranians have virtually no memory of the Islamic Revolution or of the monarchical regime that preceded it. Their focus is on the future, and many appear to want the same freedoms and rights that young people in the democratic West enjoy. Whether demographic trends will gradually help push Iranian society toward more openness—or whether religious conservatives will maintain a great degree of control—remains to be seen.

ECONOMIC OVERVIEW

For most of its history, Iran's economy was based on nomadic herding and agriculture. The harsh weather and limited water resources of the Iranian plateau were not suitable for growing crops, so the inhabitants of this region survived by herding animals from one area to another, depending on the season and the level of rainfall. The animals not only provided food, but also were used for making carpets, clothing, and tents. Because a nomadic lifestyle is conducive to living in groups, the early Iranians formed large tribal confederations, which became the foundation of the Persian dynasties.

In the earliest years, agriculture in Iran was limited to oases and the few regions of the country that received significant rainfall. But around 1000 BCE, Iranians developed an ingenious system of

Vendors in Tehran's bustling Grand Bazaar sell a wide variety of goods. Iran's merchant class, known as the *bazaaris*, dates to the Sasanian era.

underground canals, known as *qanats*, that carried water from mountain streams to the arid land below. Farmers would dig wells to tap into an underground canal and use the water to irrigate their fields. This allowed the people to settle in one place, which led to the creation of small villages and towns in the foothills of the mountains. Remarkably, the 3,000-year-old *qanats* are still in use today.

Under the Sasanian emperors, from the third to the sixth century, Iran's cities began to thrive. Growing cities not only benefited the agricultural regions of the country (the cities needed food supplies), they also promoted the development of industries and trade. It was during this period that a merchant class first appeared, based in the cities' teeming **bazaars**. To this day, Iran's merchants are known as *bazaaris*. Subsequent empires continued to build and expand Iran's cities, adorning them with great palaces and mosques.

But even as the cities grew, Iran's economy remained essentially agricultural until the 20th century. In the early 1900s, after oil was discovered in Iran, the economy began a slow transformation. At first, most of the revenue from Iran's oil exports went to the British firm that produced the oil and, to a lesser extent, Iran's rulers; the general population, which remained predominantly farmers and nomadic herders, saw little economic benefit.

Reza Shah, the founder of the Pahlavi dynasty, attempted to modernize Iran by expanding the educational system and improving the country's *infrastructure*. Mohammed Reza Pahlavi, who succeeded his father in 1941, accelerated the modernization effort. As oil became an increasingly important international commodity, and as Iran began to receive a greater share of oil revenues, the shah was able to spend money on the construction of factories and other industrial projects. He also continued to expand and improve the infrastructure. In 1977 the shah boldly predicted that within a decade Iran would have the same standard of living as European nations. But much of the *foreign exchange* Iran earned from its oil exports was used to buy weapons or was stolen by corrupt government officials. While the country took on an outward appearance of modernization, the majority of the people were poor, and in rural villages and urban slums life had changed very little.

The leaders of the Islamic Revolution introduced a completely different approach to economics. Their emphasis was on self-reliance, and they banned the importation of many expensive luxury goods. The Islamic Republic nationalized many industries, banks, and the transportation sector and seized land that had been held by top supporters of the shah, many of whom had fled the country. The *bazaaris* and other small-scale business owners, however, were allowed to keep their economic freedom and were a strong voice for private enterprise. Although the religious leaders argued for self-reliance, nearly 90 percent of the government's revenue continued to come from oil exports.

The eight-year war with Iraq had a devastating impact on the Iranian economy. Moreover, during the 1980s international oil prices declined sharply, which reduced Iran's revenue at the same time that its agricultural production was also falling. Ever more money had to be spent on imported food. Further compounding Iran's economic problems was the fact that many international investors questioned the stability of the Islamic government, and thus were unwilling to invest in Iran. The United States, which under the shah had been a principal investor in the country's economy, was now Iran's archenemy.

When Khatami was elected president in 1997, he faced a dire economic situation. Iran's population—which stood at more than 60 million—was growing rapidly, and the country's economy needed to grow at an annual rate of more than 6 percent just to maintain employment levels. But in the late 1990s, the economic growth rate was barely 1 percent, leading to widespread unemployment.

As of 2015, unemployment was still high—more than 10 percent, according to the *CIA World Factbook*. With an estimated 2015 gross domestic product (GDP) of $403 billion, Iran ranked 164th among the world's economies. Iran remains heavily dependent on its oil revenues, and therefore its economy is vulnerable to fluctuations in the price of oil on the international market. In income per capita (average income), Iranians fall into the lower-middle range among the world's countries. Wealth in Iran is very unevenly distributed. More than 18 percent of the country's population live in conditions of poverty, according to the latest statistics.

Several factors prevent greater economic development in Iran. To begin with, much of the economy is controlled directly by the state, and Iran's state-run industries are plagued by inefficiency and corruption. In addition, the policies of the Iranian government—for example, the regime's insistence on pursuing a nuclear program—have led the United States and other countries to limit trade with and impose economic sanctions on Iran. Foreign investment in Iran is low, and without large-scale investment from abroad, Iran will find it difficult to diversify its non-oil economic sectors.

Economic Sectors

Of the major economic sectors—agriculture, industry, and services—Iran's largest is the last. The service sector contributes about 50 percent of Iran's GDP. Important services include government, education, health care, and tourism-related services. With its great historic cities and rich culture, Iran has the potential to be a significant tourist destination, and thus to greatly expand this part of its service economy. Between 1995 and 2000, the number of tourists visiting Iran nearly tripled, with the largest number coming from Europe (of the few tourists who visit from the United States, most are Iranian-Americans with family in Iran). But as long as the Islamic Republic pursues controversial international and domestic policies, only the most adventurous tourists are likely to visit. Moreover, many of the more extreme religious conservatives among Iran's leadership fear the corrupting influence of visitors from Europe and the United States, and they actively discourage further development of tourism.

Industry accounts for about 41 percent of Iran's GDP. Within the industrial sector, petroleum production is far and away the most important component: 80 percent of Iran's estimated $96 billion in 2013 export earnings came from the sale of oil. Iran holds around 9 percent of the world's known oil reserves and around 16 percent of the world's natural gas. The petroleum industry is under full government control, with very limited private or foreign investment. Iran is an important member of the Organization of Petroleum Exporting Countries (OPEC), an economic *cartel* composed of the world's major oil exporting nations. OPEC attempts, often with only limited success, to determine the international price of oil by regulating production. Iran frequently has been at odds with Saudi Arabia, another major member of OPEC, over production levels and other issues. Since the 1920s, every Iranian government has pledged to diversify the economy to decrease dependence on petroleum—and none has achieved more than marginal success.

One-quarter of Iran's workforce continues to be employed in the agricultural sector, even though agriculture accounts for less than 10 percent of the country's GDP and Iran must import many food products. Iran's most important agricultural products are the staple grains: wheat, rice, and barley. Other important agricultural products are dates, pomegranates, figs, melons, and strawberries. Important agricultural exports include pistachio nuts and caviar from the Caspian Sea. Iran's farmers are generally poor and live in

A poor elderly man sells batteries and razors on the street near a mosque in Sanandaj. Although Iran is rich in oil resources, wealth is unevenly distributed, and many people live below the poverty line.

the villages that dot the Iranian plateau and the foothills of the mountain ranges. Increasingly, young people from these rural areas are heading to Iran's larger cities in search of better employment opportunities.

Under the shah, Iran invested billions of dollars in heavy industries in an attempt to diversify away from oil. Today, most of these industries are controlled by the government and are an important source of employment, especially in Iran's growing cities. Major industries include food processing, such as refined sugar, cooking oil, and canned goods; cement manufactur-

Iran's world-famous handmade carpets are a major non-oil export product.

ing; metal fabricating; and copper mining. Iran's state-owned automobile factories produce an estimated 750,000 vehicles per year. They include automobiles and commercial vehicles.

One of the most important and well-known industries in Iran is the production of carpets and rugs. Traditionally made by hand, carpets today are more likely to be made by machines in factories (those that still are made by hand on a loom are extremely expensive). Carpets are a major non-oil export—around one-third of all "oriental carpets" produced in the world are made in Iran—and a source of great pride for Iranians.

EARLY RELIGIONS

In ancient times, the various tribes and ethnic groups that inhabited Iran worshiped many gods and goddesses that represented forces of nature (wind, rain, lightning, and so on) or astronomical bodies (the sun, moon, and stars). Each tribe had its own set of deities.

Around 600 BCE, a charismatic religious leader named Zoroaster began preaching the existence of one supreme and omnipotent God, whom he called Ahura Mazda. Zoroaster taught that Ahura Mazda, the creator of the world and all its life, is good. However, according to Zoroaster, there also exists a force of darkness and evil (Ahriman) that tempts humans to pursue the wrong path. Zoroaster believed in a strict moral code, and he believed that every individual has the free will to decide between right and wrong behavior. Before long, Zoroaster began to attract followers, who became known as Zoroastrians. Among them was the Persian emperor Darius the Great.

Over the ensuing centuries, Zoroastrianism grew in popularity, developing a hierarchical priesthood and gradually supplanting the old tribal religions. Around 275 CE, Zoroastrianism was made the official religion of Iran under the Sasanians, and Zoroastrian priests became powerful figures behind the throne. Zoroastrianism remained the dominant religion until the introduction of Islam in the middle of the seventh century.

ISLAM

The Islamic religion was founded in the seventh century in the Arabian Peninsula by the prophet Muhammad, a merchant and trader in the city of Mecca who claimed to have received revelations from God. These revelations became Islam's sacred text, the Qur'an. Initially the Meccans rejected Muhammad's revelations, and he and his small band of followers were forced to flee to Medina. But 10 years later, with many more followers, he returned triumphant to Mecca and the new religion took hold there.

After Muhammad's death in 632, his followers rapidly spread

Islam throughout the Middle East, North Africa, and even Spain. Many people found Islam an attractive religion and converted with little struggle. By 700 Iran was under the control of the caliph of Damascus, and it has been an Islamic nation ever since.

Today, Islam is one of the world's largest religions, with more than 1.6 billion adherents stretching from Morocco to Indonesia. Many Westerners incorrectly equate Muslims (as Islam's adherents are called) with Arabs, but in fact, the largest Muslim countries in the world—Indonesia, Pakistan, India, Bangladesh, and Iran—are *not* Arab.

Muslims believe in the same God as Jews and Christians (the name "Allah" is simply the Arabic word for "God"). They acknowledge the importance of the Hebrew prophets and of Jesus, but believe that Muhammad was the final and most important prophet.

An Iranian woman wearing a hijab walks past the Imam Khomeini Mosque in Tehran.

Shiite Muslims participate in community prayers during a Friday afternoon outside the Imam Mosque in Isfahan.

To Muslims, the Qur'an, as revealed to Muhammad by God, is the guide to life. Because it is believed to be the literal word of God, and was revealed in the Arabic language, all Muslims are expected to learn to read the Qur'an in Arabic. Translations in other languages exist, but they are not considered the authentic word of God.

One of the keys to Islam's popularity is the simplicity of its practice. In addition to faithfully observing the "five pillars," Muslims are forbidden to drink alcohol or eat pork. Some Muslims also believe that a woman's face should be covered by a veil whenever she is in public.

The Muslim house of worship is known as a mosque, and in every Iranian town and city the mosque serves as a center of religious and social life. Five times a day, from every mosque in the Muslim world, comes the "call to prayer." A religious official called a *muezzin*, speaking through a loudspeaker, intones the words "God is great" (*Allahu akbar* in Arabic) to indicate that it is time for prayers. Muslims, who may pray anywhere, respond to the call by kneeling in prayer in their homes, in their offices, or even on the sidewalk. On Friday, the Islamic holy day, Muslims gather in mosques to pray and hear a reading from the Qur'an by a religious leader known as an *imam*.

SHIISM

A major rift in Islam occurred in the decades following Muhammad's death in 632. The Prophet had left no instructions on who should succeed him as leader of Islam, and two different camps emerged. The majority of Muhammad's followers supported the Prophet's close friend and adviser, Abu Bakr, as leader, or caliph. These Muslims, who believed that the caliph should be selected from among the most pious believers, became known as the Sunni, from the Arabic word for "tradition." A minority, however, favored Ali, Muhammad's cousin and son-in-law, as the new leader of Islam. They believed that leadership of Islam should pass through the Prophet's male descendants (neither of Muhammad's two sons survived childhood, but Ali was married to Muhammad's daughter Fatima). These Muslims became known as the Shia (or Shiites), from the Arabic word for "partisans." The Shia promoted Ali as the caliph for more than 20 years, but the Sunni candidate always succeeded in securing the caliphate. Finally, in 656, Ali was elected caliph. But five years into his rule he was assassinated, and when his son, Hossein, was murdered several years later, the rift between the Sunni and Shia intensified.

Today, Iran is the world's largest majority Shiite nation: approximately 90-95 percent of its population are Shiites, and 5-10 per-

Iranians walks past the entrance to the shrine of Imam Reza in Mashhad.

cent are Sunni. (Although Iran had become a Muslim country by around 700, Shiism did not become the officially recognized religion until 1500, under Safavid rule.) Other countries with large Shia populations include Iraq, Bahrain, and Lebanon. Shiism plays an extremely important role in Iranian politics and society and has often contributed to animosity between Iran and some of its Sunni neighbors, such as Saudi Arabia. Since the Islamic Revolution, Iran has worked with Shia communities in other countries to foment revolution and unrest.

OTHER RELIGIONS

Iran has small communities of Zoroastrians, Jews, and Christians. Together they account for about 1 percent of the population. Most Iranian Christians are of Armenian descent. The few Zoroastrians who remain, and who have held on to their religion for more than 1,300 years, live mostly around the city of Yazd. Jews, who have lived in Iran since the sixth century BCE, have contributed much to Iranian life and culture. At the time of the Islamic Revolution, they numbered around 80,000 and lived mostly in the major cities. In light of the revolution's extreme opposition to Israel and strict interpretation of Islamic law, many Iranian Jews fled the country for the United States, Israel, or Europe. Today, only an estimated 9,000 to 12,000 Jews live in Iran. The Jewish community is guaranteed one seat in the Majlis, and Jews can legally practice their religion unhindered, but they live under constant suspicion. In 1999 several Iranian Jews were arrested and accused of spying for Israel, despite little real evidence.

Aside from Sunni Muslims, Baha'is constitute the largest religious minority group in Iran, though the government does not recognize them as legitimate. In fact, the Baha'is, who believe that every religion is true but that theirs is the culmination of all religions, are regarded by Islam as a heretical sect, and are subject to persecution and oppression. Hundreds of Baha'is have been imprisoned or executed since the Iranian Revolution. The Baha'i faith began in Iran in the 19th century. In the mid-1980s, Baha'is claimed 350,000 Iranian adherents. Since then, many have tried to leave the country to escape persecution.

 ## Text-Dependent Questions

1. What is the most powerful political position in Iran?
2. When did Ayatollah Khomeini die?
3. What category of natural resources is the basis of Iran's international economic impact?

 ## Research Project

Read about the events inside Iran during the 1970s that culminated in the overthrow of the shah and the rise to control of Ayatollah Khomeini. Write a report for your teacher.

Colorfully dressed Turkmen children pose for a photograph. The Turkmen, a traditionally nomadic people of Turkic origin, make up about 2 percent of Iran's population. Of Iran's many ethnic groups, Persians form the largest; 61 percent of the country's people are of Persian ancestry.

The People

Iran's history is one of empires and invasions. Located at the crossroads of Arabia, central Asia, and Turkey, Iran has incorporated many different cultural, ethnic, and linguistic influences throughout its history. The majority of Iranians are of Indo-European ancestry, descended from the early tribal groups that moved into the Plateau of Iran from central Asia around 1000 BCE. Sometimes known as Aryans, these groups include Persians (who make up roughly 50 percent of the population today), Kurds, and Baluchis.

A common mistake is to consider Iran an Arab country. It is not. Iran has a small Arab minority (around 2 percent of the population, living mostly in the southwest along the border with Iraq), but the majority Indo-Europeans are more closely related to Indians, central Asians, and even Europeans than they are to Arabs and other **Semitic** groups. Other significant ethnic groups include Azeris (about 16 percent of the population), who are of Turkic origin and live primarily in northwest Iran, and Kurds (about 10 percent of the population), who live in the west along the borders with Turkey and Iraq. Iran is home to small populations of Armenians, Turkmen, and Jews.

Despite this ethnic mixture, most people consider themselves to be Iranian whatever their origins. In recent history, only the Kurds have periodically expressed **separatist** desires, part of a larger movement with the Kurds of Iraq, Turkey, and Syria to create an independent Kurdish state. But other ethnic groups, such as the Baluchis from southeastern Iran, complain of discrimination.

LANGUAGES

The official language of Iran, spoken by about 53 percent of the population, is Farsi (sometimes called Persian). Farsi is an Indo-European language. It is written in the Arabic script and, like Arabic, read from right to left on the page. But Farsi is not linguistically related to Arabic, even though many Arabic words have entered into the language. Within Iran, various dialects of Farsi are spoken (just as various dialects of English are spoken across the United States). The dialect spoken in and around Tehran is the most widely known as it is more commonly heard on television and radio broadcasts. But all Farsi speakers are mutually intelligible.

Many Iranians speak a primary language other than Farsi, and

 Words to Understand in This Chapter

Aryans—any of several Indo-European tribes, including the Persians, Kurds, and Baluch, that migrated to the Plateau of Iran from central Asia around 1000 BCE.

calligraphy—the art of writing words in beautiful or stylized lettering.

chador—a heavy black cloak covering nearly all of a woman's body.

Semites—any of a group of peoples of Middle Eastern origin, including Arabs and Jews, who speak Semitic languages.

separatist—expressing a desire to separate.

As this map shows, most of Iran's population is concentrated in the north and west of the country.

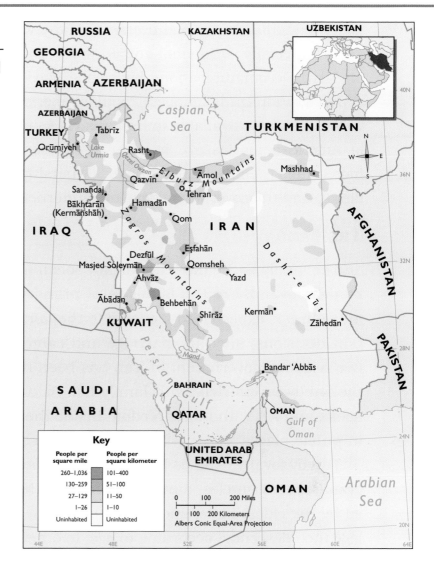

some do not speak Farsi at all. Around one-quarter of the population speaks one of the Turkic languages (Azeri and Turkmen), and the Kurdish population speaks mostly Kurdish. Arabic is spoken by the small Arab community, but it is understood by millions of others, since Arabic is the official language of the Qur'an and all students of religion—and devout Muslims—must learn to read Arabic.

Increasingly, many Iranians speak English or another European language, such as German. Some older professionals, such as doctors, studied or trained overseas. Many younger Iranians, especially university students, are eager to learn foreign languages. Modern telecommunications has made it easier for Iranians to be exposed to foreign languages. Popular American and European television shows are available to Iranians via satellite dishes, videotapes of American movies are in wide circulation, and the Internet is increasingly popular. Still, private ownership of satellite dishes is illegal, and the government regulates Internet use.

THE FAMILY

The family is the most important social institution in Iran. The honor and unity of the family is of primary importance, and an individual is expected to conform to the family's wishes on important decisions, such as marriage and career. Even the conservative religious government of Iran has been reluctant to intrude on the family or interfere with family life. As a result, Iranians often speak and act with more freedom inside their homes than they do in public places.

Family loyalty extends beyond one's immediate family to include grandparents, uncles, aunts, and cousins. Most families are headed by the eldest male, such as a grandfather. Authority and privilege then descends, according to age, to other males. Women do not exert power or authority within the family, at least not openly. Behind the scenes, however, a respected female family member may have considerable influence.

Family gatherings are a primary social activity in Iran. Families always get together for meals on holidays, and they frequently eat together on Fridays, the Islamic day of worship. Even young people rarely go out on their own for entertainment, especially since the Islamic Revolution, which imposed more conservative structures on society. Instead, families go out in groups for picnics, walks through the park, or movies.

Men have traditionally enjoyed far greater freedom in Islamic societies than have women. Even inside the home, women and men usually ate separately and gathered in separate rooms to talk or watch television. In the 1960s and 1970s, under the shah, Iran experimented with granting women greater freedoms. Many urban women entered the workforce, and some became important professionals and government officials. One of the goals of the Islamic Revolution

Iran's 1979 revolution brought gender segregation, a traditional practice in Islam, to many facets of public life, including education. Shown here are a teacher and her students at a girls' primary school in Tehran. By law all Iranian girls and women age nine and older must wear conservative Islamic dress when in public.

led by the Ayatollah Khomeini was to reestablish the more traditional Islamic relationship between men and women.

Since the revolution, women's rights have been greatly restricted.
Segregation of the sexes has become more widespread: in schools,
workplaces, and even on public buses, men and women are separated. Many restaurants have separate rooms for women and families.
By law, any girl over the age of nine must wear conservative Islamic
dress when in public, such as the ***chador*** (a black cloak that covers
the entire body except for the face). In general, as little of a woman's
body as possible should be visible to strangers.

But Iranian women enjoy many rights that women in other
Islamic countries do not have. They can vote and run for office, for

Quick Facts: The People of Iran

Population: 80,840,713 (rank 19th in the world).
Ethnic groups: Persian 61%, Azeri 16%, Kurd 10%.
Religion: Islam (official), 99.4%; Zoroastrian, Jewish, Christian, other 0.6%.
Languages: Persian (official) 53%, Azeri Turkic and Turkic dialects 18%, Kurdish 10%, Gilaki and
    Mazandarani 7%, Luri 6%, Balochi 2%, Arabic 2%, other 2%.
Age structure:
    0–14 years: 23.7%
    15–24 years: 18.7%
    25–54 years: 46.1%
    55–64 years: 6.3%
    65 years and over: 5.2%
Population growth rate: 1.22% (rank 97th in the world).
Birth rate: 18.23 births/1,000 population (rank 105th in the world).
Death rate: 5.94 deaths/1,000 population (rank 168th in the world).
Infant mortality rate: 39 deaths/1,000 live births (rank 55th in the world).
Life expectancy at birth: 70.89 years (rank 149th in the world).
Literacy: 86.8% (2015 est.).

All figures are 2014 estimates unless otherwise indicated.
Source: Adapted from CIA World Factbook, 2015.

example (although the constitution states that only a man may serve as president). They are allowed to drive cars, own property, and be out in public at any hour of the day or night (as long as they are properly attired, of course). More women than men are enrolled in Iran's universities, and women may become professionals in most fields. Nevertheless, women's rights is a growing issue in Iran—many young Iranian women, in particular, are speaking out for change—and the Islamic Republic has also received much criticism from international human rights groups on this subject.

Because women and men are segregated, dating and marriage in Iran are completely different from dating and marriage in the West. Many Iranian marriages are arranged—that is, the two sets of parents decide that their children will get married. Often the bride and groom are complete strangers to each other. Prominent families will try to ensure that their children marry the children of other prominent families. An Iranian marriage is not considered a union of equals—the husband has full authority in the relationship, and the newly married couple become part of the husband's extended family. According to Shia religious law, a man may marry up to four wives simultaneously. This very rarely occurs, however, because the husband is supposed to provide for his wives and all their children, and few Iranians have enough money to support more than one household.

Over the past 50 years, Iran has undergone a major social transformation as large numbers of people moved from rural areas and villages to the larger towns and cities. Today, 83 percent of Iranians live in urban areas (compared with 31 percent in 1956). This transformation has had an important impact on family life and has worked to weaken some of the traditional customs. In cities, people occupy smaller houses and apartments, making it hard at times for all members of an extended family to live in close proximity. By contrast, some small villages in Iran may consist of only a few extended families, all living and working together. Moreover, the urban environment has made it easier for younger Iranians to meet each other outside of the family context.

IRANIAN CUISINE

Classical Iranian cuisine (often called Persian cuisine) is one of the great cuisines of the world. Iranian dishes usually include fresh fruits and vegetables, a range of meats, and seafood, rice, and bread. The key ingredients, however, are the many aromatic herbs and spices used in Iranian recipes, such as sumac, saffron, mint, and coriander leaves. Even the simplest dish, such as a bowl of fresh yogurt, may be enhanced with diced cucumbers and fresh mint leaves.

Iran's most famous dish is kabob—pieces of marinated beef, lamb, or chicken on skewers, cooked over hot coals. Ground meat (like hamburger) and fish can also be used for kabob, and a vege-

An array of foods laid out for Nowruz, the traditional Persian New Year celebration.

tarian version can be made with fresh vegetables. Kabob is served over rice or wrapped in a piece of thin, fresh hot bread called *nan*. In major cities and towns, virtually every street has one or more small food stalls, known as *kabobis*, serving nothing but kabob and canned soft drinks. *Kabobis* are very popular with working people, students, and others who want a quick and inexpensive lunch.

Iranian families normally eat fairly simple meals that emphasize rice, bread, and vegetables; meat, which is more expensive, is served frequently but is generally not the main focus of the meal. Popular vegetables are spinach, squash, and eggplant. *Nan* is served with every meal, and even in the poorest homes it is made fresh daily. At home, it is common for families to sit on the floor and eat on low tables, which are covered with an embroidered tablecloth. Picnicking is a very popular family pastime, and in nice weather city parks fill up quickly.

For larger or more festive meals—such as on holidays or at big family gatherings—more elaborate dishes are served. *Khoresh*, a thick and delicious stew, is one of the most popular. It is a combination of meat (lamb, beef, or veal), poultry, or fish with vegetables, beans, and sometimes fruits and nuts. Herbs and delicate spices are always added, and the dish then cooks over low heat for many hours in a large stew pot. If made by a good cook, the combination of flavors in a *khoresh* dish makes for a unique culinary experience. An example would be lamb with butternut squash and prunes, spiced with cinnamon, saffron, and lime juice. *Khoresh* is usually served over mounds of rice.

Other popular Iranian dishes include vegetables stuffed with meat and rice (*dolmeh*), and *kuku*, a large fluffy omelet stuffed with vegetables, cheeses, or meats. Yogurt is served with most meals, and the diner often mixes it with his or her rice. Nuts, fruits, and various pickles are widely available, inexpensive, and popular as snacks. For dessert, Iranians normally have fruit (fresh or dried) or homemade rice or saffron pudding.

The Islamic religion strictly forbids the consumption of alcoholic beverages, and since the Islamic Revolution alcoholic drinks have been banned from Iran except for use by the Christian minority. Locally bottled soft drinks are popular, as are fresh fruit juices, milk shakes, and a drink made from sour cherry syrup. *Dugh* is a refreshing drink made with yogurt and club soda, topped with fresh mint leaves. Iran's national drink is hot tea (called *chai*), served black in a small glass without handles. Iranians have mastered a unique way of sweetening their tea: they take a small sugar cube, hold it between their teeth, and then sip the tea through their teeth! (Foreigners are allowed to simply place the sugar cube in the glass of tea.) Every Iranian city or town has numerous teahouses, where men can meet to drink tea, smoke, and socialize.

EDUCATION

Until the Pahlavis came to power in Iran in 1926, very little attention was paid to education. Those who wished to pursue a religious education could attend a religious school and learn to read the Qur'an, and very wealthy Iranians had access to private teachers or foreign education. But for the average Iranian prior to the 20th century, formal education was not a realistic possibility.

Reza Shah Pahlavi came to power with the desire to make Iran a modern nation-state, and education was one of his top priorities. As more oil wealth began to accrue to the government throughout the mid-20th century, more income was available to build schools and universities and train teachers. The leaders of the Islamic Revolution have maintained the emphasis on education, although with a more religious focus and with the segregation of male and female students beginning in primary school.

The emphasis on education has paid off. As recently as the 1940s, very few Iranians could read or write. Today, the overall literacy rate is about 91 percent for men and 83 percent for women; it is even higher among the urban population. The University of Tehran, established in 1934, was Iran's first modern state university. By 1978 Iran had 22 state universities, and by 2014 there were 98 state universities and another 33 private institutions of higher education.

A school for the training of Sunni clerics in southern Iran. Iran's Sunni Muslims make up less than 10 percent of the population and tend to be ethnic Arabs living in border areas such as Khuzestan province.

Today, primary-school education is available for free to all students, boys and girls, and is compulsory beginning at age six. Almost all six-year-olds are enrolled in school. At the end of each year, students must pass an exam in order to proceed to the next grade. The primary-school cycle ends at fifth grade, at which time students must take a national exam in order to proceed to the middle-school cycle.

Middle school covers grades 6 to 8. Students are required to study English beginning in grade 7 (otherwise, all instruction is in Farsi). By the end of their middle-school years, students must decide whether they will pursue an academic education or a technical/vocational education. An academic education could be in literature, economics, mathematics, or the sciences. A technical/vocational education would emphasize specific job skills in preparation for the labor market. Once again, students must pass an exam at the end of middle school in order to proceed to secondary school.

In secondary school (grades 9 through 12), students follow either an academic curriculum or a technical/vocational curriculum. They must pass a nationwide exam at the end of each year of secondary school in order to proceed. Those who choose the technical/vocational curriculum will enter the workforce after secondary school. Those who pursue the academic curriculum may continue to a university or a teacher-training institute.

Despite the progress of recent decades, Iran faces many challenges in its educational system. One is the demand for higher education, which greatly exceeds the number of places available in universities and colleges. In 1987, the Iranian government began offering distance education at Payame Noor University. With Internet advances, students can receive instruction online.

Many wealthy Iranians still send their sons and, increasingly, their daughters overseas for higher education. Compounding the problem of higher education is that there often are no good jobs available for those who do attend and graduate from universities. Many of those who study overseas find jobs in their host country and do not return to Iran. This loss of educated, talented citizens is referred to as Iran's "brain drain."

Another challenge facing Iranian leaders is the gap that still exists between education in rural areas and education in cities. Students in rural areas and small towns suffer from poorer schools and fewer opportunities for higher education. Iran is also struggling to incorporate more technology, such as the Internet, into its school system. A small number of schools in major cities are connected to the Internet, but the majority of schools have only limited techno-logical resources.

Finally, many young people in Iran today want to see less emphasis on religious education and more on skills and knowl-edge that will prepare them for the modern world. In some cases, student protests on university campuses have demanded greater intellectual freedom and defended professors who have come under attack from religious conservatives.

THE ARTS AND LITERATURE

The Iranian people have made significant contributions to the arts since the time of the ancient Persian empires. Perhaps the greatest contribution has been in architecture: Iran's cities are a showcase for some of the finest and most beautiful examples of mosques, palaces, and other monumental buildings. Because Islam forbids the depiction of the human form, architects adorned their buildings with colorful tiles or mosaics of intricate geometric and floral designs. Another means of decorating buildings was with *calligraphy*—beautifully stylized Arabic writing of passages from the Qur'an. The golden age of Persian architecture came during the time of the Safavid ruler Shah Abbas I (1587–1629). His royal capital, Isfahan, is a living museum of architecture.

Another art form for which Iran is world-famous is the "Persian miniature"—a small, delicate, and colorful painting depicting a scene from traditional literature, stories, or poems. Miniature painting began in the 15th century and is still practiced by Iranian artists. Many of the finest older examples, however, are in European and American museums.

Iran has a rich and ancient musical tradition. Classical Persian music involves the singing of traditional poems, accompanied by musicians on stringed instruments, drums, and flutes. Each of the many different ethnic groups that make up Iran has its own traditional folk music, passed down over the centuries. Today, young Iranians enjoy Western pop

A man plays a traditional Iranian musical instrument. Iran's various ethnic groups all have their own distinctive styles of folk music.

music, although such music can be hard to find, and it is not always advisable to listen to it in public places. Iranian pop music is also popular, but the musicians and singers must be very careful not to offend Islam or the principles of the Islamic Revolution. In the face of hostility from the government, some of the most famous Iranian pop musicians (especially women singers) have left the country and only perform overseas, usually before large audiences of fellow expatriate Iranians.

Iran's greatest contribution to world literature has been its poetry. Classical Persian poems were very long (they were known as epic poems). The most famous Persian poet was Omar Khayyám, who lived in the 11th and early 12th centuries. His epic poem *Rubaiyat* was translated into English and has had a great impact on Western poets. Another great Persian poet, known simply as Ferdosi, lived in the 10th century. His epic *The Book of Kings* is still read by Iranians. Ferdosi insisted in writing only in Farsi at a time when there was great pressure to introduce Arabic; many Iranians credit Ferdosi with saving the Farsi language.

Unfortunately, little Iranian fiction has been translated into Western languages, so the work of Iranian novelists and short-story writers remains unknown to most of the world. Sadeq Hedayat and Simin Daneshvar are two modern Iranian authors whose works have been translated into English.

In the immediate aftermath of the Islamic Revolution, religious conservatives attacked both the Iranian film industry, for being un-Islamic, and the country's cinemas, for showing decadent foreign films. The Revolutionary Guards burned down hundreds of cinemas, and many film directors and actors either fled the country or gave up their profession. By the 1990s, however, Iran had gained a reputation for producing excellent films. Several have won awards at major international film festivals and have been well received in Europe and the United States. As more reform-minded officials gained power (President Khatami served as minister of culture in the 1990s), Iranian directors gained more freedom to explore issues and topics that are not always discussed openly in Iran. For example, Jafar Panahi's *The White Balloon* (1995) follows a young girl walking through the streets of Tehran, where she encounters a number of unscrupulous and shady characters. *Taste of Cherry*, a film directed by Abbas Kiarostami that won the 1997 Palme d'Or prize at the prestigious Cannes Film Festival in France, deals with suicide, an issue that is normally taboo in Muslim society. Kiarostami's 2002 film *Ten* deals with women's issues and was shown in the New York Film Festival.

In the first years of the new century, a number of Iranian films have received high marks at international film festivals. They include dramas, musical comedies, and documentaries.

Despite the relative freedom that film directors have been given, their films still must pass through a strict government approval process. Every year many films are censored, purportedly because they portray life in a way that would be offensive to devout Muslims.

ENTERTAINMENT

Entertainment for most Iranians means spending time with their families, going to the cinema or a favorite restaurant, watching videos with friends in the privacy of their homes, or—for men—meeting with friends at teahouses (in the larger cities, some teahouses are beginning to serve both men and women). Because religious authorities have banned alcohol, there are no bars, and because men and women are not allowed to socialize together (at least not in public), there are no discos or nightclubs. Playing card games is illegal because it may encourage betting, which is forbidden in Islam (chess was initially outlawed for the same reason, but it became legal again by special decree in 1989). However, the sanc-

Members of Iran's national soccer team pose for a photo before a qualifying game for the 2015 Asian Cup tournament. Iran has won the Asian Cup three times, in 1968, 1972, and 1976. Soccer is Iran's most popular spectator sport.

tity of the Iranian home means that some banned activities are still enjoyed out of public view. Possessing alcohol, however, is a serious criminal offense.

The most popular spectator sport is soccer. Professional teams play before large crowds and television audiences from October to June. Tehran's Azadi Stadium, the site of many matches, holds more than 100,000 fans. Iran's national soccer team is a source of great pride. The team has qualified for the World Cup four times (1978, 1998, 2006, and 2014) but have never advanced past the group stage. Iran's only win in the World Cup tournament was a 2–1 victory against the United States in 1998.

 ## Text-Dependent Questions

1. What is the official language of Iran?
2. What is the word for the black robe Iranian women must wear?
3. In what grade are Iranian students required to study English?

 ## Research Project

Look into the history and art form of calligraphy. Create a calligraphy presentation for the class, and be prepared to explain the origins of the intriguing style of lettering.

Pedestrians walk past the Fatima Masumeh Shrine in Qom, which Shiites consider to be one of the most sacred cities in Iran.

Communities

I ran's great cities have been important centers of commerce, politics, and ideas for centuries. Today, a majority of Iranians live in cities, most of which have grown rapidly over the past 50 years. This growth has brought change, but at their cores, Iran's great cities retain their unique identities and embrace their fascinating histories.

TEHRAN

Tehran's emergence as an important city came relatively late. It began as a village at the foothills of the Alborz Mountains. Descriptions of Tehran written in the 11th century report that its people lived in underground dwellings and survived through basic agriculture and highway robbery. In the 12th century, Mongol attacks against neighboring villages caused many of their residents to move to Tehran, which gradually became a prosperous trading and market town.

In the 16th century, Tehran's beautiful natural setting at the base of the mountains and its plentiful water supplies came to the attention of the Safavid king, Tahmasp I. He ordered that walls and gates be built around the city and constructed elaborate gardens and new buildings. In 1785 the Qajar king Agha Mohammed Khan declared Tehran his capital and immediately began constructing buildings and palaces. But Tehran remained essentially a small town and grew only slowly during the 19th century.

The 20th century saw explosive growth. As Iran evolved into a unified nation, Tehran became an increasingly important capital and commercial center. Meanwhile, more and more Iranians moved from rural areas to cities in search of work, and Tehran was transformed almost overnight: its population rose from 300,000 in 1930 to 1.8 million in 1956. Twenty years later, in 1976, the city's population had grown to 4.5 million; by the early years of the 21st century, Tehran was home to more than 12 million, making it one of the 20 largest cities in the world. This growth was accompanied by the construction of large government buildings; apartment houses; new streets and squares; and schools, universities, museums, and hospitals. Today, Tehran is not only Iran's capital, but also its economic, industrial, and academic center. In addition, it serves as the country's transportation hub, with Iran's largest airport and busiest train and bus terminals.

Tehran's rapid growth has not come without problems. Foremost among them is pollution, primarily from automobiles (it is estimated that half of all cars in Iran belong to Tehranis). On

 Words to Understand in This Chapter

cosmopolitan—worldly, with an international atmosphere of sophistication.
teahouse—a cafe where customers enjoy tea and light refreshments.

View of Tehran, the capital and largest city. Milad Tower, built in 2007, rises 1,427 feet (435 m) above the city.

hot summer days, air pollution becomes so serious a problem that many residents flee the city for the mountains to the north, where the air is clear and cool. On particularly bad days, the government issues health warnings and closes schools to help ensure that children stay indoors. A related problem is traffic: Tehran's roads are notoriously chaotic and, especially for pedestrians, downright dangerous. Tehran's public bus system is extensive, but the buses are crowded and slow. The city's subway system is modern, safe, and fast, but it has only nine stations and does little to relieve automobile traffic.

Not surprisingly, Tehran's rapid and uncontrolled growth has spawned overcrowding and poverty. The southern part of the city, in particular, is teeming with recent immigrants from the country-side who live in dilapidated apartment buildings. The northern part of the city, home to Tehran's wealthier residents, is more pleasant and less congested. The far northern suburbs approach the Alborz Mountains, and numerous trails lead out of northern Tehran into the mountains.

Tehran lacks the magnificent architecture of some of Iran's other cities—in fact, many people consider its more modern architecture drab and boring. But Tehran does boast a number of interesting cultural attractions. The National Museum of Iran contains archaeological exhibits from all parts of the country. The Golestan Palace, a complex of museums and other buildings situated in a beautiful garden, was built in the 19th century by a Qajar ruler who had traveled to Europe and been impressed by the palaces of European royalty. One of the more interesting sites in Tehran is the former U.S. embassy, in which 52 American diplomats and support staff were held hostage for 444 days during the immediate aftermath of the Islamic Revolution. Among Iranians the building is known today as the "U.S. Den of Espionage."

ISFAHAN

Isfahan (population 1.9 million) is one of the most magnificent cities in the Islamic world. It is the masterpiece of Shah Abbas the Great, who came to power in 1587 and unified the nation after driving out the last of the Mongol invaders. Shah Abbas was determined to have a capital city that was unrivalled in the world. He chose Isfahan, located on the Plateau of Iran just to the east of the Zagros Mountains.

Isfahan served as the seat of the Safavid Empire for only about a century. But during that time, beautiful mosques, palaces, and bridges were built, and they still stand today. The fact that the capital was moved from Isfahan—first to Shiraz, and then to Tehran—was a blessing in disguise, for it helped the city avoid the uncontrolled growth that has plagued Tehran, making it that much eas-

Mosaic tiles in floral and geometric patterns, as well as calligraphy, adorn the dome of the splendid Imam Mosque in Isfahan. The mosque was begun in 1611, during the reign of the Safavid ruler Shah Abbas I.

ier to enjoy its architectural wonders.

The center of Isfahan is a great square built in 1612 and known today as Imam Khomeini Square, after the leader of the 1979 Islamic Revolution. This huge square, which measures about 1,600 feet (488 meters) by 400 feet (122 meters), is lined with small shops and features a large rectangular pool with fountains at its center. At one end of the square is the Imam Mosque, completed in 1629 and regarded as one of the grandest mosques in the Islamic world. Its large dome is covered with beautiful tiles painted with floral and geometric designs and adorned with calligraphy. On either side of the square stand the Sheikh Lotfollah Mosque, smaller than the Imam Mosque but equally impressive in its decoration, and the Ali Qapu Palace, which served as Shah Abbas's seat of government. Both were built in the early 17th century. In another part of Isfahan is the Jame Mosque, the largest mosque in Iran and also one of the oldest, having been completed in 1121.

Isfahan is renowned for five old bridges that span the Zayandeh River, which runs through the middle of the city. Most of these bridges were built in the 17th century and are closed to traffic. They have **teahouses** at either end that are popular meeting places for both Isfanhanis and the city's many tourists.

Isfahan once had a large Armenian Christian population, but most have left. Thirteen churches remain, however, including the very large and well-maintained Vank Cathedral, completed in 1655, which towers over the city's Christian quarter.

Isfahan's residents often shop in the city's bazaar, one of the largest and oldest in Iran. The bazaar features hundreds of merchants selling everything from household goods to exquisite Persian carpets, local handicrafts, food, and spices. One can easily become lost in its confusing system of narrow pathways and alleys.

Contrasting with the beauty of central Isfahan are the city's outskirts, which are marred by heavy industry (mostly steel plants) and lower-income housing. Pollution from the factories and automobiles sometimes spreads over the entire city.

SHIRAZ

Shiraz, a city of about 1.3 million people, is located in the south-central part of the country in a fertile valley on the western slopes of the Zagros Mountains. Its elevation of nearly 5,000 feet (1,525 meters) gives it a pleasant climate, with mild winters and comfortable summers. Shiraz holds a special place in the hearts of Iranians, who regard it as their cultural capital (it was also briefly the political capital, from 1747 to 1779). A **cosmopolitan** city, Shiraz is known for its poets, its gardens, and, before the Islamic Revolution, the wonderful wine that was made from the grapes of nearby vineyards. Its population surged during the war with Iraq, when thousands of refugees fled from the border areas.

Shiraz was first settled more than 2,500 years ago, but it did not become an important city until around 700 CE, after the Arab Islamic invasion. For several hundred years it was ruled by Arabs, after which a succession of local Iranian dynasties held power. The city grew steadily—and actually flourished—under the Mongols, who conquered and ruled Iran in the 13th and 14th centuries but spared, and even favored, Shiraz. It was during this period that Shiraz began to attract artists, poets, and scholars. Its reputation grew as well, and it was soon regarded as one of the most important cities in the Islamic world.

Iranians still consider the work of two poets who lived in Shiraz during the 13th and 14th centuries to be Persia's greatest contributions to literature. The poet known as Saadi, who died in 1292, wrote beautiful love poems that many Iranians today learn by heart. His two most famous poems are called *The Garden of Roses* and *The Garden of Fruits*. Saadi's tomb, surrounded by a garden, is a major tourist attraction in Shiraz. The Iranian custom is to touch the marble tomb while reciting a prayer to Saadi. Shiraz's other great poet, known as Hafiz, lived from 1300 to 1389. His poetry was more religious and mystical in nature, and he too is popular among Iranians today. It is said that in many Iranian homes, there are only two books: the Qur'an and a copy of Hafiz's poems. Hafiz also is buried in Shiraz, and his tomb is another popular site for visitors.

After enjoying its golden age in the 13th and 14th centuries, Shiraz went into a long decline that lasted several hundred years. In 1749, however, Karim Khan, ruler of the Zand dynasty, made Shiraz his capital and devoted himself to transforming it into a great city again. He built dozens of new buildings and mosques and constructed a magnificent bazaar that remains to this day the commercial center of the city. But in 1779 the new Qajar dynasty rulers moved the capital to Tehran. Shiraz, however, was firmly established as the country's cultural heart.

Today Shiraz is an administrative and regional commercial center, as well as a major tourist destination for Iranians and foreign visitors alike. In addition to the tombs of its two great poets, Shiraz is known for its tree-lined boulevards and its many beautiful mosques and gardens. Most attractive is the 19th-century Garden of Paradise, a perfect place to sit and read the poetry of Saadi and Hafiz. Another attraction just outside Shiraz are the ruins of the great ancient city of Persepolis, the capital of Cyrus the Great's Persian Empire.

MASHHAD

With a population of around 2.4 million, Mashhad is Iran's fourth-largest city. More important, however, it is an extremely sacred city to Shiites throughout the world, and a major pilgrimage center. Mashhad means "Place of the Martyr," and Shiites believe that it is where the eighth imam—a direct descendant of the prophet Muhammad—died in 817, reportedly poisoned by the Sunni caliph. Millions of devout Shiites visit Mashhad every year to pray and grieve at the holy shrine of the eighth imam. The shrine is in fact an entire walled compound, containing museums, mosques, several theological colleges, and libraries.

Mashhad is located in Iran's harsh northeast, less than 100 miles (161 km) from the borders with Afghanistan and Turkmenistan. In winter, heavy snowfalls are common. Throughout history, its location has made it subject to invasion and periodic influxes of refugees fleeing crises in neighboring countries.

Because of its sacred importance, Mashhad has been favored by the Islamic Republic and has benefited from large infusions of government funds. The year-round presence of devout religious pilgrims and the large number of local clergy give the city an austere and somber atmosphere.

OTHER CITIES

Among Iran's other important cities are Tabriz, in the far northwestern part of the country; the holy city of Qom; and Yazd, one of the world's oldest cities. Tabriz has a fascinating history. In the third century CE, it was the capital of Azerbaijan. Sacked by the Mongols in the 14th century, it was ruled for a short time by Turkish tribes before serving very briefly as the capital of Persia early in the Safavid dynasty. Twice during the 20th century the city was occupied by Russia. It is best known today for its incredible 15th-century bazaar, which contains more than 7,000 shops and over 2 miles (3.2 km) of narrow passages and lanes.

Qom is a small city, but second only to Mashhad in religious importance. It is located in central Iran, about 100 miles (161 km) south of Tehran. The Ayatollah Khomeini lived and taught in Qom before being forced into exile by the shah in the 1960s. Qom remains a center of religious conservatism and pilgrimage.

Yazd is an ancient city located at the very edge of the Iranian desert. Its old quarter has mud-brick homes and buildings that date back to the Sasanian era (224–642 CE). In the 13th century, Yazd lay along the Silk Road and was visited by Marco Polo. Yazd also was the center of the Zoroastrian religion, and it is still home to the largest Zoroastrian population in Iran.

HOLIDAYS AND CELEBRATIONS

The biggest holiday in Iran is Nowruz, the traditional Persian New Year, which predates the introduction of Islam. In the immediate aftermath of the Islamic Revolution in 1979, the clergy attacked the Nowruz celebrations but quickly realized that the holiday was far too popular to suppress. Nowruz lasts for two weeks during the period of the spring equinox in March. It is a holiday of family gatherings, feasts with special holiday dishes, and gifts for children. Parties last far into the night, with singing, music, and poetry readings (usually of Hafiz). Many urban residents return to their ancestral villages as schools and offices close. As some of the traditions of Nowruz date back many centuries, their origin is often unknown.

For example, it is customary to build bonfires in public places and invite friends to leap over them while simultaneously shouting wishes for good fortune in the coming year. Children dress as ghosts and spirits and go from door to door, beating pots and pans and asking for treats. Traditional food during Nowruz includes fish and noodles—both of which are believed to bring good luck—and wonderful pastries and sweets.

The other major holiday in Iran is Ramadan, the traditional Muslim month of fasting and the most important holiday in Islam. During Ramadan, Muslims refrain from eating, drinking, or smoking during daylight hours. The purpose of this fast is to cleanse the body and soul and to create empathy with those who are less fortunate. Religious police roam the streets during Ramadan to make sure that no one is violating the fast (non-Muslims are exempt from fasting, as are pregnant women, the sick, and the elderly). Because the Islamic calendar is based on the moon's cycles, Ramadan falls on different dates from year to year. If it lands in the hot and dry summer, when days are long, people can become irritable and exhausted observing the fast; as a result, many businesses and government offices close or operate on shortened hours.

During Nowruz, Iranians jump over bonfires for good luck in the coming year.

Once the sun goes down, however, people are free to eat and drink again, and families gather to pray and celebrate their successful completion of a day of fasting. The last day of Ramadan is a major holiday in itself. Known as Eid al-Fitr (Festival of the Breaking of the Fast), it is celebrated with great feasts and boisterous parties to culminate Islam's most sacred month.

Other religious holidays include Ashura, which commemorates the death of Hossein, the third Shiite imam; the birthday of Muhammad; and the anniversary of the death of the Prophet's daughter Fatima. Other national holidays include the anniversary of Ayatollah Khomeini's triumphant return to Iran, the anniversary of the establishment of the Islamic Republic, and the anniversary of Khomeini's death. On the latter day, hundreds of thousands of Iranians descend on Tehran and Qom to pay homage to Khomeini and pray at sites associated with his life.

 ## Text-Dependent Questions

1. In what city did the Ayatollah Khomeini live and teach before he was forced into exile in the 1960s?
2. What Iranian holiday is similar to Halloween, when children engage in a form of trick-or-treating?

 ## Research Project

Write a report about Ramadan, the Islamic holy month. What are the requirements and restrictions people must obey? Describe the traditional activities that take place on Eid al-Fitr, the last day of Ramadan.

(Top) Iranian officials (seated at right) participate in talks in Geneva, Switzerland, with representatives from France, Germany, the United Kingdom, China, Russia and the United States on Iran's nuclear program In April 2015, Iran agreed to accept significant restrictions on its nuclear program and to allow international inspections. (Bottom) In recent years Iran has been the closest ally of Syrian dictator Bashir al-Assad, and has provided military and technical support to prop up the regime during the civil war that began in 2011.

Foreign Relations

The Persian Empire was one of the great powers of the ancient world. Its struggles against the Greeks, Romans, Mongols, and Ottoman Turks helped determine the course of history for many centuries. Even after the Arab invasion and the conversion to Islam, Iran maintained its identity and culture and pursued its own national interests in the region. As the world's leading Shiite Muslim nation, Iran always had a unique sense of mission and purpose within the Muslim world.

Iran's role on the world stage diminished with the rise of the great European powers. But the importance of its strategic geographical position has never changed, and in the 19th and early 20th centuries Iran became the target of European intrigue and influence, especially during the two world wars. As awareness of Iran's vast oil resources grew, Iran emerged as an even more coveted prize among the European powers. Unlike much of the non-European world, however, Iran was never directly colonized or controlled by Europeans. Its identity as a nation, its borders, and its sense of importance in the region remained strong.

After World War II, Iran cast its lot with the United States and the West in the struggle against Soviet communism. Iranians were motivated in part by fear of Soviet expansion—after all, Iran shared a long border with the Soviet Union and had suffered from Russian invasions in the past—and in part by a desire to more fully integrate its economy with that of the prosperous Western nations. Unfortunately, under the Pahlavi shahs Iran's pro-Western foreign policy was combined with authoritarian rule at home. While Iran had a long history of authoritarian dynastic rule, the Pahlavis did not appreciate the changing social and political dynamics of the late-20th-century world. The Iranian people demanded changes in the way they were governed. The resulting Islamic Revolution that overthrew the shah also dramatically changed Iran's foreign policy, breaking its strong ties with the West while simultaneously redefining its regional role.

FOREIGN POLICY OF IRAN: THE EARLY YEARS

After the birth of the Islamic Republic in 1979, the most remarkable element of its foreign policy was its extreme anti-Americanism. Ayatollah Khomeini and the other leaders of the revolution believed that the shah had been able to maintain his rule for so long only because of U.S. support and financial assistance. Moreover, despite

 Words to Understand in This Chapter

atheism—the belief that God does not exist.
domestic—living inside a city or country.
radical—possessing and acting on extreme political and social opinions.

A young Iranian at an anti-American demonstration. After he came to power in 1979, the Ayatollah Khomeini labeled the United States—which had been a major supporter of the shah—"the Great Satan." Two decades later, U.S. president George W. Bush declared that Iran was part of an "axis of evil."

U.S. assurances to the contrary, they feared that the United States was working behind the scenes to reinstall the shah. Khomeini regularly referred to the United States as "the Great Satan." The new revolutionary government also found that having a powerful foreign enemy helped it secure internal authority and gave it an excuse to suppress any **domestic** opposition.

Some officials in the revolutionary government believed that a full rupture with the United States was a bad idea. They still wanted U.S. investment, and they still feared Soviet intentions. More **radical** elements in the government, however, wanted to break all ties with "the Great Satan." These officials encouraged the November 1979 assault on the U.S. embassy in Tehran by a gang of demonstrating students, and they supported the students for more than a year as they held the American hostages. In the end, the radicals won out (some of the officials who had argued for maintaining ties with the United States were jailed and executed). The result was a complete severing of relations between the two countries and the introduction of an era of U.S.-Iranian mistrust and hostility that continues into the 21st century.

Relations with the other Western nations also became strained under the revolutionary government, although Iran demonstrated much less hostility toward Europe than it did toward the United States. Iran's revolutionaries also were hostile to the Soviet Union—which Khomeini termed "the Lesser Satan"—because of the Soviets' official policy of **atheism** and their antagonism toward all religions. When the Soviet Union invaded Afghanistan in 1979, Iran was harshly critical and offered support to the Afghan resistance fighters (as did the United States).

In its early years, the Islamic Republic sought not only to break from the United States but also to "export" Islamic revolution to other countries in the Middle East. Iran's government began to support, through various direct and indirect means, a number of revolutionary Islamic organizations in other Middle Eastern countries, especially those enjoying close relationships with the United States. Most important among these was Lebanon, whose sizable Shiite minority inhabited much of the southern part of the country, near the border with Israel. Iran began to support radical Lebanese Shiite organizations, especially a group called Hezbollah. When Israel invaded Lebanon in 1982, Iran took the opportunity to offer further aid to Hezbollah, and it even sent a small contingent of Iranian troops to Lebanon to help fight the Israelis.

Hezbollah also targeted the United States. Two deadly terror attacks in Lebanon were traced to Hezbollah and thus to Iran. In the first attack, a bomb at the U.S. embassy in Lebanon's capital of

Beirut killed 63 people; several months later, 241 U.S. Marine peacekeepers were killed when a truck laden with explosives drove into their barracks. In addition, a number of American citizens in Lebanon were kidnapped and held hostage during the 1980s by groups that were aided by Iran. These actions by Iranian-supported terrorist groups served to further inflame U.S.-Iranian relations.

Iran's policy of exporting its revolution stirred great fear in neighboring states. Several Arab countries in the Persian Gulf region, including U.S. allies Saudi Arabia and Bahrain, were home to Shiite minorities. In the aftermath of the Iranian Revolution there was a notable increase in terrorism and other subversive acts in these countries, and the perpetrators often were linked to Iran. Perhaps the Arab state that most feared Iranian intervention was Iraq. Though ruled by a Sunni Muslim, Saddam Hussein, Iraq was actually a majority Shiite nation. Fearing that Iran would attempt to mobilize Iraqi Shiites against his regime, and wanting to strike while Iran was still unstable, Saddam Hussein launched an invasion of Iran in 1980. The ensuing war, which lasted eight years and killed perhaps a million people on both sides, greatly depleted Iran's resources and thus prevented the revolutionary government from more active involvement in neighboring states. It also intensified Iranian hostility toward the United States, which Iran's leaders correctly perceived as being supportive of Iraq.

Under the shah, Iran was one of the few Islamic nations in the world to maintain diplomatic relations and conduct extensive trade with Israel. Upon seizing power, the leaders of the Iranian Revolution immediately denounced the relationship and cut all ties with Israel. The Ayatollah Khomeini argued that Israel was an illegitimate state that should be eradicated. He and other leaders of the revolution condemned any Arab governments (such as Jordan and Egypt) that advocated compromise and reconciliation with Israel, and supported those (such as Syria and Libya) that took a hard-line position on the question of Arab-Israeli peace.

Iran's hostility toward Israel, however, did not prevent the Islamic Republic from purchasing weapons from the Jewish state in 1985 during the height of the war with Iraq. This purchase was part of secret three-way negotiations among Iran, Israel, and the United States over the U.S. hostages held in Lebanon. The deal created a major scandal in the United States when it was uncovered and investigated by Congress.

IRANIAN FOREIGN POLICY IN THE 1990s

During the 1990s Iran began to put less emphasis on exporting revolution, in part because after 10 years this had not proved a very successful policy (no other Middle Eastern nation had become an Islamic republic, and only in Algeria were Islamic forces threatening to succeed). Moreover, even the most radical Iranian leaders understood the need to devote energy and resources to rebuilding the country after the war with Iraq. Iran's leaders also were beginning to realize that their policies had largely isolated Iran—which carried a significant economic cost, as foreign investment had been scared off.

When Iraq invaded Kuwait in 1990, precipitating the U.S.-led Persian Gulf War that expelled the Iraqis from Kuwait the following year, Iran stayed on the sidelines. It denounced both Iraq, for invading Kuwait, and the United States, for intervening militarily in the crisis.

In 1993 U.S. president Bill Clinton adopted a policy of "dual containment" toward Iran and Iraq—in other words, the United States would attempt to contain both countries and treat them as equally hostile to U.S. interests in the region. In the face of continuing evidence that Iran supported international terrorist organizations, was pursuing the development of nuclear weapons and long-range missiles, and actively opposed the U.S.-brokered Middle East peace process, President Clinton imposed new economic and trade sanctions against Iran in 1995.

In 1996 a bombing at a U.S. military base in Saudi Arabia killed 19 U.S. servicemen; as in earlier terrorist incidents, Iran was once again linked to the terrorist organization that conducted the attack. In response, the U.S. Congress passed a law penalizing any company—American or foreign—that invested money in Iran's oil and gas sector. The European Union challenged this law and vowed not to observe it.

As Iran started to focus more on its internal struggles—in particular, the contest between conservatives and reformists—its foreign policy gradually shifted and softened. It sought to improve ties with European states and its Arab neighbors (except for Iraq, toward which Iran remained hostile). After the election of the reformist Khatami as president in 1997, a more concerted effort was made to break Iran out of its isolation. Khatami visited Italy and France in 1999—the first visit by an Iranian leader to a Western nation since before the revolution—and even met with Pope John Paul II. These visits and other openings to the Europeans succeeded in generating more European investment, something Iran's battered economy desperately needed.

President Clinton expressed cautious optimism about Khatami's election, but he insisted that U.S. policy toward Iran would not change as long as Iran supported terrorist groups, tried to hinder the Arab-Israeli peace process, and worked on developing nuclear weapons. In an interview in 1998, President Khatami proposed the establishment of cultural exchange programs between the United States and Iran to "break the walls of mistrust." However, he ruled out any formal government-to-government ties. Secretary of State Madeleine Albright proposed that the two countries work to establish normal relations again. In 1999 the United States eased slightly the array of economic sanctions against Iran.

IRAN'S FOREIGN POLICY SINCE 2000

Iran's foreign policy continues to be driven as much by internal tensions between reformists and conservatives, pragmatists and hard-liners, as by any actions of foreign countries. For example, while President Khatami was quick to publicly condemn the September 11, 2001, terrorist attacks against the United States, Supreme Leader Khamenei blamed U.S. policies for the attacks—which, incongruously, he also claimed were probably masterminded by Jewish supporters of Israel. Despite these mixed signals, Iran cooperated with the United States in Afghanistan, which U.S. and allied forces invaded in October 2001 to pursue the al-Qaeda terrorist organization responsible for the September 11 attacks and to topple Afghanistan's Taliban government, which sheltered al-Qaeda.

In the ensuing months, several public statements pointed to increased tensions between the United States and Iran. In January 2002 U.S. president George W. Bush called Iran part of an "axis of evil." In May of that year Supreme Leader Khamenei said that negotiating with the United States for an improvement in relations would be a waste of time and "would not solve any problem."

But behind the scenes, American officials and reformists within the Iranian government were discussing possible approaches to normalizing relations between their respective countries. In April 2003—a few weeks after the United States had launched an invasion of Iraq—an Iranian proposal for a "grand bargain" was transmitted to Washington. In exchange for concessions such as an end to all sanctions against Iran and an American pledge not to seek the overthrow of Iran's government, the Iranians reportedly offered to put all major areas of U.S. concern on the table. These included Iran's nuclear program, its sponsorship of terrorism, and its support for anti-Israel organizations such as Hamas and Hezbollah. Some American officials believed that Iran's hard-liners would prevent

Iranian president Hassan Rouhani (right) speaks with President Fuad Masum of Iraq at a 2014 conference. Once implacable enemies, Iran and Iraq have forged closer relations in recent years—a development that concerns some of the United State's closest allies in the Middle East, including Saudi Arabia and Israel.

President Khatami and his moderate allies from following through on any grand bargain, and some U.S. officials were not persuaded of the authenticity of the message, which was delivered indirectly, through the mediation of the Swiss government. Additionally, U.S. forces appeared to have won a quick and decisive victory in Iraq, and some members of the Bush administration seem to have believed that the United States had no need to compromise with Iran. Ultimately, the administration chose to ignore the Iranian grand bargain overture.

The situation in Iraq soon turned chaotic, however. American forces found themselves trying to suppress a Sunni Arab insurgency, to battle foreign terrorists who had entered Iraq, and to stop murderous violence between Iraq's Sunni Arab and Shiite communities. U.S. military commanders and members of the Bush administration accused Iran of arming and training Shiite militias that targeted American troops, and even of deploying members of the Revolutionary Guards' elite Quds Force directly to Iraq.

Mahmoud Ahmadinejad's election in 2005 as Iran's president augured growing tensions between Washington and Tehran. Ahmadinejad's anti-Israel rhetoric, combined with Iran's ballistic-missile and nuclear programs, greatly alarmed Israeli leaders as well. During the summer of 2006, Israel fought a brief but destructive war in southern Lebanon against the Iran-sponsored radical group Hezbollah.

In 2007—confronted with what it said was continuing Iranian involvement in fomenting violence in Iraq, as well as Iranian support of extremist groups throughout the Middle East—the Bush administration designated Iran's Revolutionary Guards Corps a "global terrorist." This designation paved the way for the United States to move against the financial assets and business operations of the Revolutionary Guards. It might also, some analysts suggested, be a prelude to war with Iran. The Revolutionary Guards are, after all, part of the Iranian government.

Yet the Bush administration did not launch a war against Iran. Furthermore, Bush's successor, President Barack Obama, announced his willingness to engage with the Islamic Republic. In a video message to Iran's people released during Nowruz festivities in March 2009, Obama called for a "new beginning" in U.S.-Iranian relations.

Hopes for engagement grew dimmer with the outcome of Iran's 2009 presidential election. The reelection of Ahmadinejad was widely denounced as a fraud, prompting violent protests throughout Iran. The government responded with a harsh crackdown on demonstrators, hundreds of arrests, and a ban on independent journalists. Foreign leaders, including President Obama, condemned the crackdown.

Entering the second decade of the century, Western nations including the United States, Canada, and the European Union imposed tight sanctions against Iran's oil exportation. Diplomatic relations were strained over Iran's nuclear development program and support of Islamic terrorist organizations. Iranian leaders dismissed foreign concerns as Western propaganda.

In 2013, Hassan Rouhani, a reformist cleric, was elected president of Iran. He proclaimed that Iran had no intentions of ever manufacturing nuclear warheads. Five world powers—the United States, Great Britain, Russia, China, Germany, and France—began a series of negotions with Iran to lift sanctions in exchange for curtailments in Iran's nuclear program. The outline of an agreement was announced in April 2015. Meanwhile, Rouhani indicated that Iran would support the government of Iraq in combatting Sunni extremists in that country.

 ## Text-Dependent Questions

1. During the Cold War after World War II, which side did Iran take?
2. What caustic term did Ayatollah Khomeini regularly voice to describe the United States? What term did he apply to the Soviet Union?
3. What reformist cleric was elected president of Iran in 2013?

 ## Research Project

Write a timeline chronicling the warm/cold diplomatic relations between Iran and Western nations, beginning with the Iranian Revolution in 1979. Examples: its stance regarding the Persian Gulf War; President Khatami's visits to Italy and France in 1999; Iranian leaders' statements about the September 11, 2001, terrorist attacks against the United States; and recent negotiations involving trade sanctions and nuclear development.

CHRONOLOGY

Ca. 1000 BCE	Indo-European tribes, including Persians, move into Iran.
Ca. 550 BCE	Cyrus the Great establishes Persian Empire.
522 BCE	Darius the Great becomes ruler of Persia.
331 BCE	Alexander the Great defeats Persian forces.
260 CE	Sasanian ruler Shapur I defeats the mighty Roman Empire in battle.
Ca. 570	Birth of the prophet Muhammad in what is today Saudi Arabia.
700	After a series of battles, Islamic forces secure control over Iran.
1219	The Mongol leader Genghis Khan invades Iran.
1501	Beginning of the Safavid Empire (which lasts until 1722), during which Shiism is established as state religion.
1587–1629	Reign of Shah Abbas.
1795	Introduction of the Qajar dynasty.
1906	Iran's first parliament is established.
1907	Russia and Britain sign an agreement to divide influence in Iran between them.
1909	Establishment of Anglo-Persian Oil Company.
1925	Establishment of the Pahlavi dynasty under Reza Shah Pahlavi.
1941	British and Russians invade Iran after Reza Shah declares his neutrality in World War II; Reza Shah is forced into exile and replaced by his son, Mohammed Reza Pahlavi.
1951	Iran's parliament nationalizes the oil industry.
1953	U.S.-sponsored coup overthrows Mossadeq government and reinstates the shah.
1963	Shah launches "White Revolution" to modernize Iran.
1972	President Richard Nixon visits Iran and establishes strong U.S.-Iran military partnership with the shah.
1979	Islamic Revolution forces shah into exile, and Ayatollah Khomeini takes over as "Supreme Leader" of Iran; Iranian students take U.S. diplomats in Tehran hostage.
1980	Iraq launches war against Iran.
1989	Ayatollah Khomeini dies.

CHRONOLOGY

1997   Iranian people elect a reformist candidate, Mohammed Khatami, to the presidency.

2001   Khatami reelected in a landslide.

2002   U.S. president George W. Bush calls Iran part of an "axis of evil."

2003   U.S. officials renew charges that Iran is trying to develop nuclear weapons; claiming that its nuclear program is peaceful, Iran vows to expand its nuclear power industry.

2004   After the Council of Guardians disqualifies thousands of reformist candidates, conservatives win control of Iran's parliament.

2005   Hard-liner Mahmoud Ahmadinejad is elected president of Iran.

2006   In July and August, the extremist group Hezbollah and Israel fight a war in southern Lebanon. Iran provides missiles and other advanced weapons to Hezbollah for this conflict. The United Nations Security Council votes to impose sanctions on Iran for that country's nuclear program.

2007   Ahmadinejad announces that Iran has the capability to produce large quantities of nuclear fuel. In June, Iranians protest their government's rationing of gasoline. The United States imposes new sanctions on Iran beginning in October.

2008   Conservatives gain more than two-thirds of the seats in parliament after the Council of Guardians again disqualifies many reformist candidates.

2009   On June 12, about 40 million Iranians vote in the presidential election. Mahmoud Ahmadinejad is declared the winner, but widespread suspicions of fraud trigger massive protests. The government responds with a brutal crackdown.

2010   In September, a powerful computer virus called Stuxnet is detected in computers at the Bushehr nuclear plant. Most experts believe Stuxnet was created by a nation-state—possibly the United States or Israel—and introduced into Iranian computer systems to slow the country's progress toward developing fuel for a nuclear weapon.

2011   International nuclear analysts warn that Iran is conducting research toward developing a nuclear warhead. Civil war begins in Syria, one of Iran's closest allies, and the Iranian government responds by providing weapons and training to help prop up the regime of Bashir al-Assad.

2012   Inspectors with the International Atomic Energy Agency (IAEA) leave Iran after being denied access to the Parchin site, south of Tehran. In July, the European Union begins a boycott of Iranian oil exports in an attempt to place economic pressure on the regime to stop enriching uranium at its Fordo facility.

2013   Hassan Rouhani, a reformist, is elected president of Iran.

2014   Russia agrees to build up to eight nuclear reactors in Iran, in a move meant to ease Iranian demands to enrich uranium. Iran and world powers conduct negotiations to end sanctions in return for Iran curbing its nuclear development program. With neighboring Iraq facing civil war and an assault from the ISIL organization, Rouhani sends Iranian Revolutionary Guards units to provide training and advice to Iraq's military and security forces.

2015   In April, Iran agrees to accept significant restrictions on its nuclear program and to allow international inspections, in exchange for an easing of sanctions from the six major powers involved in the talks: France, Germany, Great Britain, Russia, the United States, and China.

SERIES GLOSSARY

autonomy—the right of self-government.

BCE and CE—an alternative to the traditional Western designation of calendar eras, which used the birth of Jesus as a dividing line. BCE stands for "Before the Common Era," and is equivalent to BC ("Before Christ"). Dates labeled CE, or "Common Era," are equivalent to Anno Domini (AD, or "the Year of Our Lord").

caliphate—an Islamic theocratic state, in which the ruler, or caliph, has authority over both the spiritual and temporal lives of his subjects and all people must obey Islamic laws.

civil society—the sum total of institutions, organizations, and groups promoting social and civic causes in a country (for example, human rights groups, labor unions, arts foundations) that are not funded or controlled by the government or business interests.

colonialism—control or domination by one country over an area or people outside its boundaries; the policy of colonizing foreign lands.

ideology—a system of beliefs, values, and ideas forming the basis of a social, economic, or political philosophy.

Islamist—a Muslim who advocates the reformation of society and government in accordance with Islamic laws and principles.

jihadism—adherence to the idea that Muslims should carry out a war against un-Islamic groups and ideas, especially Westerners and Western liberal culture.

nationalism—the belief that shared ethnicity, language, and history should form the basis for political organization; the desire of people with a common culture to have their own state.

Pan-Arabism—a movement seeking to unite all Arab peoples into a single state.

self-determination—determination by a people of their own future political status.

Sharia—Islamic law, based on the Qur'an and other Islamic writings and traditions. The Sharia sets forth the moral goals of an Islamic society, and governs a Muslim's religious political, social, and private life.

Shia—the smaller of Islam's two major branches, whose rift with the larger Sunni branch originated in seventh-century disputes over who should succeed the prophet Muhammad as leader of the Muslim community.

Sunni—a Muslim who belongs to the largest branch of Islam.

Wahhabism—a highly conservative form of Sunni Islam practiced in Saudi Arabia.

Zionism—the movement to establish a Jewish state in Palestine; support for the State of Israel.

Berlatsky, Noah, ed. *The Iranian Revolution*. San Diego, Calif: Greenhaven Press, 2012.

Downing, David. *Iran*. New York: Marshall Cavendish, 2008.

Esposito, John. *What Everyone Needs to Know About Islam*. New York: Oxford University Press, 2002.

Etheredge, Laura S. *Iran*. New York: Rosen Publishing Group, 2011.

Hiro, Dilip. *The Longest War: The Iran-Iraq Military Conflict*. New York: Routledge, 1991.

Kenney, Karen. *Iran*. Edina, Minn.: Essential Library, 2011.

Kheirabadi, Masoud. *Iran*. New York: Chelsea House Publishers, 2011.

Mansfield, Peter. *A History of the Middle East*. 4th ed. revised and updated by Nicholas Pelham. New York: Penguin Books, 2013.

Nardo, Don. *The Persian Empire*. San Diego: Lucent Books, 1998.

Schemenauer, Elma. *Welcome to Iran*. Mankato, Minn.: Child's World, 2008.

Schwedler, Jillian. *Understanding the Contemporary Middle East*. Boulder, Colo.: Lynne Rienner Publishers, 2013.

Sick, Gary. *All Fall Down: America's Tragic Encounter with Iran*. Authors Guild, 2001.

Spyer, Jonathan, and Cameron Brown. *The Rise of Nationalism: The Arab World, Turkey, and Iran*. Philadelphia: Mason Crest, 2007.

Stern, Jessica, and J.M. Berger. *ISIS: The State of Terror*. New York: Ecco, 2015.

INTERNET RESOURCES

http://www.state.gov/p/nea/ci/ir/

The U.S. State Department website has a thorough section on Iran, including background information on its economy, politics, and other information.

https://www.cia.gov/library/publications/the-world-factbook/geos/ir.html

The CIA World Factbook website provides a great deal of statistical information about Iran and its people. It is regularly updated.

www.mideasti.org

An extensive resource geared to educate Americans about the Middle East. This academic site includes loads of information for research.

www.un.org/english

The English-language web page for the United Nations can be searched for Iran-related stories and information.

www.bbc.com/news

The official website of BBC News provides articles and videos on important international news and events related to the Middle East and elsewhere.

www.aljazeera.com

The English-language website of the Arabic news service Al Jazeera provides articles and videos on breaking news, as well as feature stories that provide background material, including profiles of leaders and essays reacting to major events.

www.fpri.org

The website of the Foreign Policy Research Institute includes informative essays by FPRI scholars on events in the Middle East.

Numbers in **bold italic** refer to captions.

INDEX

INDEX/PICTURE CREDITS

page
2: © OTTN Publishing
3: Thomas Koch / Shutterstock.com
12: Wojtek Chmielewski / Shutterstock.com
16: Javad Montazeri
18: used under license from Shutterstock, Inc.
19: © OTTN Publishing
22: used under license from Shutterstock, Inc.
24: Charles & Josette Lenars/Corbis
28: (top) Nader Davoodi
28: (bottom) Lloyd Cluff/Corbis
30: Roger Wood/Corbis
33: Stapleton Collection/Corbis
34: Roger Wood/Corbis
38: Hulton-Deutsch Collection/Corbis
43: Javad Montazeri
45: National Archives
47: U.S. Department of Defense
51: United Nations photo
52: used under license from Shutterstock, Inc.
55: © OTTN Publishing
56: Bettmann/Corbis
59: Shepard Sherbell/Corbis Saba
60: AFP/Corbis
61: United Nations photo
64: Shepard Sherbell/Corbis Saba
68: Radiokafka / Shutterstock.com
69: Javad Montazeri
71: Radiokafka / Shutterstock.com
72: used under license from Shutterstock, Inc.
74: Matyas Rehak / Shutterstock.com
76: Javad Montazeri
79: © OTTN Publishing
81: David Turnley/Corbis
84: Paul Almasy/Corbis
87: Javad Montazeri
90: Javad Montazeri
92: Almonfoto / Shutterstock.com
94: Giancana / Shutterstock.com
97: used under license from Shutterstock, Inc.
99: Dave Bartruff/Corbis
104: Javad Montazeri
106: United Nations photo (top); Valentina Petrov / Shutterstock.com (bottom)
109: Javad Montazeri
115: United Nations photo

Senior Consultant CAMILLE PECASTAING, PH.D., is acting director of the Middle East Studies Program at the Paul H. Nitze School of Advanced International Studies at Johns Hopkins University. A student of behavioral sciences and historical sociology, Dr. Pecastaing's research focuses on the cognitive and emotive foundations of xenophobic political cultures and ethnoreligious violence, using the Muslim world and its European and Asian peripheries as a case study. He has written on political Islam, Islamist terrorism, social change, and globalization. Pecastaing's essays have appeared in many journals, including *World Affairs* and *Policy Review*. He is the author of *Jihad in the Arabian Sea* (Hoover Institution Press, 2011).

The FOREIGN POLICY RESEARCH INSTITUTE (FPRI) provided editorial guidance for this series. FPRI is one of the nation's oldest "think tanks." The Institute's Middle East Program focuses on Gulf security, monitors the Arab-Israeli peace process, and sponsors an annual conference for teachers on the Middle East, plus periodic briefings on key developments in the region.

Among FPRI's trustees are a former Undersecretary of Defense, a former Secretary of the Navy, a former Assistant Secretary of State, a foundation president, and numerous active or retired corporate CEOs, lawyers, and civic leaders. Scholars affiliated with FPRI include a Pulitzer Prize–winning historian; a former president of Swarthmore College; a Bancroft Prize–winning historian; and a former Ambassador and senior staff member of the National Security Council. And FPRI counts among its extended network of scholars—especially its Inter-University Study Groups—representatives of many diverse disciplines, including political science, history, economics, law, management, religion, sociology, and psychology.

WILLIAM MARK HABEEB is a professor and international affairs consultant in Washington, D.C. He specializes in Middle East politics and conflict resolution. He has written widely on such topics as international negotiation, the politics and culture of North African states, and the Arab-Israeli conflict. He received his PhD in international relations from the Johns Hopkins University School of Advanced International Studies.